T0350986

Frontend Development

Frontend development is the process of creating user-interactive components. User interfaces, buttons, user-entered data, webpages, and user experience (UX) features are all examples of frontend development.

User experience is the primary focus of frontend development. As frontend engineers, you build the portions of an application that are directly accessed by end users using relevant coding and design approaches with the goal of making the overall interface elegant, easy to use, fast, and secure, fostering user engagement and interaction. Frontend development is the process of transforming data into a graphical user interface. The essential foundations of frontend web development have always been HTML, CSS, and JavaScript.

Anyone interested in becoming a frontend developer has a bright future ahead of them. Increased Internet usage, particularly on mobile devices, necessitates more user interfaces, resulting in more frontend developer jobs. The role of frontend web developers is more crucial than it has ever been.

Key Features:

- A step-by-step approach to problem-solving and skill development

- A quick run-through of the basic concepts in the form of a "Crash Course"

- An advanced, hands-on core concepts with a focus on real-world problems

- An industy-level coding paradigm, practice-oriented explanatory approach

- A special emphasis on writing clean and optimized code, with additional chapters focused on coding methodology

Frontend Development

The Ultimate Guide

Sufyan bin Uzayr

CRC Press
Taylor & Francis Group
Boca Raton London New York

CRC Press is an imprint of the
Taylor & Francis Group, an **informa** business

First edition published 2023
by CRC Press
6000 Broken Sound Parkway NW, Suite 300, Boca Raton, FL 33487-2742

and by CRC Press
4 Park Square, Milton Park, Abingdon, Oxon, OX14 4RN

CRC Press is an imprint of Taylor & Francis Group, LLC

ISBN: 9781032312958 (hbk)
ISBN: 9781032312941 (pbk)
ISBN: 9781003309062 (ebk)

DOI: 10.1201/9781003309062

Typeset in Minion
by Deanta Global Publishing Services, Chennai, India

Contents

Acknowledgments

There are many people who deserve to be on this page, for this book would not have come into existence without their support. That said, some names deserve a special mention, and I am genuinely grateful to:

- My parents, for everything they have done for me.

- My siblings, for helping with things back home.

- The Parakozm team, especially Divya Sachdeva, Jaskiran Kaur, and Vartika, for offering great amounts of help and assistance during the book-writing process.

- The CRC team, especially Sean Connelly and Danielle Zarfati, for ensuring that the book's content, layout, formatting, and everything else are perfect throughout.

- Reviewers of this book for going through the manuscript and providing their insight and feedback.

- Typesetters, cover designers, printers, and everyone else, for their part in the development of this book.

- All the folks associated with Zeba Academy, either directly or indirectly, for their help and support.

- The programming community in general, and the web development community in particular, for all their hard work and efforts.

Sufyan bin Uzayr

Author

SUFYAN BIN UZAYR IS a writer, coder, and entrepreneur with more than a decade of experience in the industry. He has authored several books in the past pertaining to a diverse range of topics, ranging from History to Computers/IT.

Sufyan is the Director of Parakozm, a multinational IT company specializing in EdTech solutions. He also runs Zeba Academy, an online learning and teaching vertical with a focus on STEM fields.

Sufyan specializes in a wide variety of technologies, such as JavaScript, Dart, WordPress, Drupal, Linux, and Python. He holds multiple degrees, including ones in Management, IT, Literature, and Political Science.

Sufyan is a digital nomad, dividing his time between four countries. He has lived and taught in universities and educational institutions around the globe. Sufyan takes a keen interest in technology, politics, literature, history, and sports, and in his spare time, he enjoys teaching coding and English to young students.

Learn more at sufyanism.com.

CHAPTER 1

Crash Course in Frontend Development

IN THIS CHAPTER

> ➤ How does the web work

> ➤ Introduction to web development

> ➤ Frontend development

> ➤ Advantages and disadvantages

This chapter will discuss frontend development and its major concepts. We will learn how websites work and what frontend development is. We will also talk about the major concepts in frontend development and the advantages and disadvantages. We will also look at the syntax and the code basics of the frontend.

HOW DOES THE WEB WORK

The web is everywhere. Before diving into frontend development and learning more about it is important to know how the web works exactly. The web is not just limited to websites that you visit. It is so much more than that. Knowing how the web works before entering into the world of web development and precisely frontend development is a crucial step.

DOI: 10.1201/9781003309062-1

What Is the Internet and How It Works

The Internet is a global system of connected computers that use TCP/IP, also called the Internet Protocol Suite, to communicate. The Internet is mainly a network of networks. It carries a vast range of information and services like email, file sharing, etc. The Internet can be considered the infrastructure, and the web is a service built on top of that infrastructure. The Internet started as a part of a research project for the United States Army in the 1960s. This research project evolved as many public universities and private companies joined the network. The public infrastructure of the Internet that we access today came into being in the 1980s. Simply put, the Internet is a way to make all the computers connected no matter what happens.

For two computers to connect, we need to link them. This link could be made physically or wirelessly. Physical links are usually done with an Ethernet cable, whereas wireless links happen through Bluetooth or Wi-Fi. All modern computers are capable of sustaining both of these types of connections.

A computer network, on the other hand, is not confined to simply two computers. You are free to connect as many computers as you like. But connecting multiple computers can get complicated real fast. Each computer that is available on the network is connected to a tiny computer called a router to solve this issue. A router acts as an intermediary or a middle man between a network of computers. It ensures that a message transmitted from a computer reaches its right destination computer. For example, Computer A wants to send a message to computer B; computer A will first send the message to the router. The router will then forward the message to computer B and ensure it does not get accidentally sent to computer C.

The Internet is an interconnected web of billions of computers, so how do we connect all of them? We connect computers to routers, routers to another router, and scale infinitely. Now that we have connected so many computers, how do we communicate with them? To send messages from our network to another network, we need to connect our network to an ISP. ISP stands for Internet service provider. An ISP is a company that has some special routers. These routers are all linked together, and they can also access the routers of other ISPs. So, if you send a message from computer A, it will get carried from your network through the network of ISP networks and will reach the destination network. The Internet is just a collection of multiple different networks like these.

Intranets and Extranets

Intranet refers to private networks that a particular organization can only access. They are used to share resources, collaborate, and communicate among members of that organization.

Extranets are similar to Intranet; the only major difference is that they are open to all or part of a private network that helps in collaborating with other organizations. They are mostly used to share information safely and securely with members like clients or stakeholders. The function of Extranet is almost the same as Intranet, like sharing files, collaborating, discussion boards, etc.

Both Intranet and Extranet almost have the same kind of infrastructure like the Internet. They also happen to use the same protocols. Members from different physical locations can also use them.

How a Website Works

Let's start with how a website works. The moment you enter a website's address into the search bar of your browser, a lot of things happen at once, and that too at lightning speed. There are so many processes that work in tandem just to view a web page. Firstly, the URL that you entered gets resolved. The request for the web page you searched for reaches the server of that particular website. The server sends a response to your request, and then the server's response is parsed. The page is then rendered and displayed to the client.

We can break down the working of websites into four steps. Each of these steps could further be divided into multiple other steps, but we will get a brief overview for now.

1. **Resolving a URL:** The website code for the URL that you enter into the search bar needs to be fetched from another computer where the data is stored. The other computer from where the data is fetched is the server. The server is a computer containing website code or the data of the website that we are looking for. The user identifies the website using a domain name, wikipedia.com. A special type of server on the Internet is called the name server or the DNS server. The DNS server's job is to convert domain names into IP addresses. A device on the Internet is identified by its IP address, which is a unique address. We will learn more about IP addresses in a while.

2. **Sending Requests:** The browser sends a request to the server with the IP address of the website that you were searching. A request usually contains a bunch of information that the browser puts together and sends that data package created to that IP address. This data is sent via HTTP, which stands for Hypertext Transfer Protocol. It is a standardized protocol that helps define what the request and response should look like. HTTP also decides which data should be included and in which form, and how the request should be submitted. This process and format of sending and receiving requests are standardized, so the server readily reads and handles the request. Afterward, based on the request, the server sends a response that is quite similar to the request. The response contains data, metadata, and the code required to render the requested page.

3. **Parsing the Server Response:** After receiving the response sent by the server, the browser parses the response. The browser first checks the data and metadata it received from the server. Based on that information, the browser decides how to display the data received from the server accordingly. If the browser receives a pdf document in response instead of a website code, it will display the pdf document in a suitable format. If the server's response contains a specific piece of metadata indicating that the response data is of type text/HTML, the browser will parse the data attached to the response as an HTML code. HTML is used for the purpose of creating the structure of any web page. HTML is a standardized language, and each HTML tag has a semantic meaning that the browser understands. The browser will parse the HTML sent through the response data. The response data is also called the response body, and it is used to render the website.

4. **Displaying the Web Page:** The browser goes through the HTML code returned by the server and renders the web page according to that. However, a website is not fully rendered after receiving a single response code. To fully render a website, a lot of additional data is fetched. Those additional requests and responses only start coming in after the first response has arrived. The HTML code sent in the first response contains the instructions to fetch more data via new

requests. The additional data could be CSS files required for the styling of the page.

TCP/IP

Transmission Control Protocol is abbreviated as TCP, and Internet Protocol is abbreviated as IP. These are nothing but a suite of communication-based protocols used to connect devices on the Internet. TCP/IP are also used as communication protocols in both Intranet and Extranet. TCP and IP are the two main protocols in the suite, but other protocols are included. The TCP/IP protocol suite acts as an abstraction layer between the Internet applications and the routing and switching fabric.

TCP/IP is used to specify how the data would be exchanged over the Internet for end-to-end communications. The protocol identifies how data should be broken into packets, transmitted, routed, and received at the destination. TCP/IP needs very little central management. It is designed to make networks reliable to recover quickly and automatically if a device on the network fails for some reason.

Both of the two main protocols of the suite serve specific functions. TCP is used to define how an application can create a communication channel over a network. TCP is also used to manage how a message gets broken down into smaller packets before transmitting them over the Internet. Those packets would get reassembled after arriving at the destination before being displayed to the client. On the other hand, IP defines how each packet would be addressed and routed to reach the right destination. Each gateway computer on the network first checks the IP address to determine where to forward the message. A subnet mask tells a network device or a computer which portion of the IP address represents the network and which portion represents hosts or any other computer on the network. The virtualization of IP addresses is done using NAT. NAT stands for Network Address Translation. NAT helps improve security and decreases the number of IP addresses an organization needs.

As mentioned earlier, TCP/IP is a suite of protocols that essentially means a collection of protocols designed to work together. Here are some of the common TCP/IP protocols:

1. **HTTP:** It stands for Hypertext Transfer Protocol, and it is used to handle the communication between a web browser and server.

2. **HTTP Secure:** This is just a secure extension of HTTP. It is abbreviated as HTTPS and securely handles communication between a web server and a web browser.

3. **FTP:** It stands for File Transfer Protocol, and it is used to handle the transmission of a file between computers.

How Does TCP/IP Work?

TCP/IP uses the client-server model of communication. In this mode of communication, another computer in the network provides a service to a client, which could be a user or a machine. The server is the other computer. Because each client request is considered a new request with no reference to the preceding request, the TCP/IP suite of protocols is classed as stateless. One of the advantages of being stateless is that it frees up the network paths to be used continuously. However, the transport layer itself is stateful. Being stateful means that after transmitting a message, the connection would remain in place until all the packets in that message have been received at the destination. After receiving, those messages are reassembled. The TCP/IP model is a little different from the seven-layer OSI model. The OSI model defines how applications can communicate over a network.

Layers of the TCP/IP Model

The TCP/IP has four layers, and each of those layers includes specific protocols.

1. **Application Layer:** This layer has applications used for standardized data exchange. The protocols available in this layer include HTTP (Hypertext Transfer Protocol), FTP (File Transfer Protocol), POP version 3 (Post Office Protocol 3), SMTP (Simple Mail Transfer Protocol), and Simple Network Management Protocol. In the application layer, the actual application data is the payload.

2. **Transport Layer:** It is responsible for maintaining end-to-end communication across the network. The protocols in this layer include TCP (Transmission Control Protocol) and UDP (User Datagram Protocol). TCP is used to handle communication between hosts. It also provides flow control, multiplexing, and reliability. TCP can be sometimes replaced with UDP for special purposes.

3. **Network Layer:** This layer is also referred to as the Internet layer. It usually deals with packets and connects independent networks to transport the packet across network boundaries. The protocols available in this layer are IP (Internet Protocol) and ICMP (Internet Control Message Protocol). ICMP is generally used to send control messages to network devices and hosts. It is also used for error reporting.

4. **Physical Layer:** This layer is also referred to as the data link layer or the network interface layer. This layer consists of protocols that operate only on a link. This is also the lowest layer, so it consists of the network component that interconnects nodes or hosts them in a network. The protocols in the layer include the Address Resolution Protocol and Ethernet for local area networks.

Advantages of Using the TCP/IP Model

- It helps in establishing a connection between different types of computers.
- It works independently of the operating system.
- It supports various routing protocols.
- It uses the client-server architecture, which is highly scalable.
- It can be operated independently.
- It is lightweight.
- It does not place any undeserved strain on a network or computer.

Disadvantages of Using the TCP/IP Model

- It is complicated to set up and manage.
- The transport layer of TCP/IP does not guarantee the delivery of packets.
- However, it is not easy to replace TCP/IP protocols.
- It is vulnerable to a synchronization attack, a type of denial-of-service attack.
- It does not separate services, interfaces, and protocols.

How Are TCP/IP and IP Different?

There are lots of differences between TCP/IP and IP. The Internet Protocol (IP) is a low-level protocol used for data communications over the Internet. The main purpose of IP is to deliver data packets with a header. The header usually consists of routing information, including the source and destination of data and the data payload itself. One limitation of IP is the amount of data it can send in one go. The maximum size of an IP data packet is between 20 and 24 bytes, including both the header and the data. This leads to multiple data packets for longer strings of data. Each packet needs to be independently sent and then reorganized again upon reaching the destination in the correct order. Also, IP is a strictly restricted protocol to only send and receive. There is no verification whatsoever about whether the data packets were sent or not.

On the other hand, TCP/IP is a communications protocol on a higher level than IP and is capable of doing more things. Even though TCP/IP still uses IP for transporting data packets from one location to another, it also connects webpages, computers, applications, and web servers. TCP understands better the stream of data required for an asset to operate appropriately and makes sure that the entire volume of that data is sent the first time. TCP also checks to ensure that the data is delivered properly at the destination source. Also, TCP can control the size and the flow rate of the data. It makes sure that the network is free of congestion that could somehow block data reception. An application wants to send a massive amount of data over the Internet. If that application only used IP, the data would be broken into multiple IP packets. Then to send those multiple IP packets, multiple requests would be made back and forth to send and receive that data because IP requests are issued per packet.

On the other hand, if that application were using TCP, it would only need a single request to send the entire data stream. TCP can also detect problems that arise in IP and even request retransmission of packets if certain data packets get lost. TCP also reorganizes packets just so they get transmitted in the proper order. This is done to minimize network congestion. Overall, TCP/IP makes transferring data over the Internet easier.

What Are Packets? How Are They Used to Transfer Data?

Packets are the basic communication unit used in a TCP/IP network. The devices available on the TCP/IP network divide the data into smaller pieces for easier transmission. Breaking down data into small pieces allows the network to accommodate various bandwidths. This helps in creating multiple routes to a single destination. In case certain pieces of data get lost or interrupted on their way to their destination, then those packets can be retransmitted. Each piece of data is considered a packet. A packet is a term that can be used interchangeably with a datagram. A packet can be seen as a smaller fragment or segment of a larger message.

History of Packets

The US government developed the Internet. The US government first conceptualized the original network that later became the Internet as an electronic network that could withstand even a nuclear attack. Then, the ideal network was thought to be something that would transmit data by changing routes dynamically. Also, if a node gets suddenly destroyed, it should be capable of identifying and retransmitting that lost data. A static and connection-oriented network was not suitable for creating such a network. It could fail very easily, as destroying even a single node would disrupt the entire chain of predetermined routes. Losing a single connection would mean the whole route would become incapable of further use. However, having a connectionless network would solve the issue because the network would stay functional no matter what. The network would simply find an alternate route to transfer the data. But for a connectionless network to work in real life, it would require small, separable units of data called packets. This is how packets came into being. They evolved due to the need for a connectionless network. It was constructed so that you do not need to establish a pre-arranged session to establish a connection. Any computer is capable of sending a network transmission out into the network. You do not need to ensure that the receiver receives the message. The US government first created ARPANET to fulfill these requirements. Then it was further developed by universities and businesses for more than two decades and then eventually renamed the Internet. The TCP/IP protocols were developed out of a common language for communication. Packets are the basic unit of data within the TCP/IP protocols.

Why Use Packets?

If we look at the scenario of transmitting data over the Internet, it could be possible to send files without dividing them into smaller packets of information. One computer could send data to another computer in the form of a long unbroken line of bits. This could be communicated as pulses of electricity that the computers can interpret. This approach was quickly deemed as a failure as a long line of bits passed over the wires could only be done by two computers. If a third computer tries to use the same wire to send the information, it would have to wait for its turn.

As this approach failed, the Internet switched to a packet switching network. Packet switching refers to the ability to network equipment to process packets independently from each other. By using this method, packets can also take different network paths to the same destination. All that matters is that they arrive at their destination. Packets from multiple computers can travel over the same wires in any order. Using packet switching allows multiple connections over the same networking equipment simultaneously. As a result of this, today, billions of devices on the Internet can exchange data over the Internet at the same time.

A packet is a string of bits that is mainly divided into three sections:

- A set of headers
- The payload, which is the actual data being transmitted
- The trailer, sometimes also referred to as the footer

The headers consist of the following:

- **Internet Protocol (IP) version**
- **Header Length**
- **ToS (Type of Service):** It is rarely used and called the Differentiated Services Code Point.
- **Size of Datagram:** The size of the header plus the payload in bytes.
- **Identification:** It is a 16-bit number. The destination computer combines the source address with the Identification to uniquely differentiate a packet. It also uses these unique identifiers to reassemble data from packets.
- **Flags:** A flag is a bit that is used to let a router know whether it can fragment a packet or not. Using a flag is important since many networks are restricted by the maximum size of packets they can forward.
- **Fragmentation offset:** A value used to help reconstruct a fragmented packet.
- **TTL (Time to Live):** The maximum number of hops a packet can take.

- **Protocol:** The type of packet, i.e., TCP, UDP, ICMP, IGMP.

- **Header Checksum:** A value used to detect errors, corruption.

- **Source Address:** The IP address where the packet originated.

- **Destination Address:** The IP address where the packet is going.

- **Options:** Rarely used.

The actual data being sent is referred to as the payload. Routers do not normally read it en route like the headers and trailers are.

In most cases, the trailer is nothing more than a pair of bits that signal the end of a packet. Occasionally, the trailer also contains CRC (Cyclic Redundancy Check) error-checking information.

Client-Server Model

The client-server model is nothing but a distributed application structure that partition tasks or workload between servers and clients. Servers are seen as the providers of a resource or service, whereas clients are seen as the service requesters. When a client computer sends a data request to the server over the Internet, the server accepts it in the client-server architecture. The data packets are returned to the client after the request has been completed. The servers do not have access to the client's resources. Examples of the client-server model are email, World Wide Web, etc.

How Does the Client-Server Model Work?

Client refers to the host computer capable of receiving information from the service providers or the servers. On the other hand, a server refers to a remote computer that provides access to a particular service. The client requests something, and the server serves it as long as it is present in the database.

Steps for Interaction between Client and Server

- The client enters the URL (Uniform Resource Locator) of the website in the browser's search bar.

- The browser would then send a request to the DNS (Domain Name System) server.

- DNS server looks up the address of the web server.

- DNS server sends a response containing the IP address of the web server.

- The browser sends over an HTTP/HTTPS request to the IP address of the web server, which is provided by the DNS server.

- The server sends all the necessary files about the original request.

- The browser renders the file with the help of a DOM (Document Object Model) interpreter, CSS interpreter, and JS engine. DOM interpreter, CSS interpreter, and JS engine are JIT (Just in Time) compilers.

- The website is displayed.

Advantages of the Client-Server Model

- It is a centralized system, and all the data is available in a single place.

- It is cost-efficient.

- It requires less maintenance cos.t

- Data retrieval or recovery is possible.

- The client and server capacities can be modified independently.

Downside of the Client-Server Model

- Clients are vulnerable to viruses, Trojans, and worms when they are available on the server or if they are accidentally posted to the server.

- Denial of Service (DoS) hacks are possible on the server.

- During transmission, data packets might be faked or manipulated.

- Phishing or obtaining login passwords or other useful user data is a typical occurrence.

- Man in the Middle (MITM) hacks are very common.

IP Address

The unique address used to identify any device on the Internet or a local network is called IP address. IP stands for "Internet Protocol." It is a set of rules and directives that govern the type of data sent through the Internet or a local network.

Essentially, IP addresses are simply used as identifiers that allow information to be sent between various devices on a network. These IP addresses contain information about the user's location and make devices accessible for communication. The Internet also requires differentiating between various types of devices like computers, mobile phones, routers, and websites. IP addresses provide a way of doing the same, and hence they act as an essential part of how the Internet works.

A numerical sequence separated by periods is the IP address and is expressed as a set of four numbers. For example, an IPv4 address might look something like this: 192.158.1.38. Each of the four numbers in this set can be anywhere between 0 and 255. As a result, the entire IP addressing range is 0.0.0.0 to 255.255.255.255. Most IP addresses that you would come across would be a set of four numbers. This type of address is symbolic of IPv4, the fourth version of IP. There is also another type of IP address named IPv6. Let's look at them and their differences.

IPv4 and IPv6

IPv4 establishes the rules used by computer networks to function based on the principle of the packet exchange. It can uniquely identify any device that is connected to the network. Whenever a device is used for Internet access, it gets assigned a unique numerical address like 195.252.149.78. The IPv4 uses a 32-bit address method. It allows it to store 2^32 addresses equivalent to 4.19 billion addresses. However, considering the steady and ever-increasing rise of Internet users, there is ongoing exhaustion of IPv4 addresses. This is why a new addressing system was created named IPv6.

Features of IPv4

- It is a protocol with no connections.
- It enables the building of a basic virtual communication layer that may be shared across multiple devices.
- It requires less memory.
- Millions of gadgets around the world currently support it.
- It offers video libraries and conferences.

IPv6, also called Internet Protocol Version 6, was first deployed in 1999, considering the increasing demand for IP addresses. IPv6 allows communication and data transfer between a network. The IPv6 uses a 128-bit address method. It allows it to store 2^128 addresses. Using IPv6 solves the problem of limited network addresses and resolves the barriers among multiple access devices to connect to the Internet. An IPv6 address looks something like this: 3ffe:1900:fe21:4545:0000:0000:0000:0000.

Features of IPv6

- It has a routing infrastructure.

- It has hierarchical addressing.

- It supports both stateful and stateless configurations.

- It provides support for QoS (Quality of Service).

- It's an excellent protocol for interacting with neighbors.

IP addresses are not generated randomly. They are mathematically produced and allocated to a user by the Internet Assigned Numbers Authority (IANA). The IANA is a division of the Internet Corporation for Assigned Names and Numbers (ICANN). ICANN is a non-profit organization, and it was first established in the United States in 1998. It was created to help maintain the security of the Internet and allow it to be usable by all. Each time anyone across the globe registers a domain on the Internet, it goes through a domain name registrar, who in turn pays a small fee to ICANN to register the domain.

IP addresses are frequently used behind the scenes, away from the users' view. The process works something like this:

- Your device gets indirectly connected to the Internet by connecting it first to a network connected to the Internet. That network then grants your device access to the Internet.

- That network is most probably your Internet service provider or ISP at home. If you are at work, you will be using your company's network.

- Your IP address keeps on changing because it is assigned to your device by your Internet service provider.

- Your Internet activity first goes through the ISP, and then the ISP would route it back to you using your IP address. Since your Internet service provider is providing you with access to the Internet, it is their role to assign an IP address to the device you are using.

- However, your IP address is bound to change based on your location. Like, for example, if you turn your router or modem on or off, it can change your IP address. Your IP address can be modified easily by just contacting your Internet service provider.

- Your home IP address.

- Does not follow you when you leave the house – for example, when you vacation – and take your device with you. This is because you will be accessing the Internet through a different network (Wi-Fi at a hotel, airport, coffee shop, etc.) and will be allocated to a different (temporary) IP address by the hotel, airport, or coffee shop's ISP.

DNS Servers

The process of DNS resolution is used to convert a hostname (such as www .example.com) into a computer friendly IP address (such as 191.178.18.71). An IP address is provided to each device on the Internet. That address is essential when it comes to finding the appropriate Internet device – just like a house address is used to find a particular house. Whenever a user wants to load a webpage, a translation must occur between what they type into their search bar in the web browser (example.com) and the machine-friendly address necessary to locate the example.com webpage that they are looking for.

To comprehend the DNS resolution process, you must first learn a variety of hardware devices that a DNS query must pass across. Besides the preliminary data request, the DNS query takes place "behind the scenes" for the browser, and it demands no involvement from the user's computer.

Four types of DNS servers are required when it comes to loading a webpage:

1. **DNS recursor:** The DNS recursor works in a similar manner as a librarian who is asked to find a particular book that is kept somewhere in the library. The DNS recursor is a server that is designed to receive queries from client machines through applications such as web browsers. Typically, the precursor is responsible for making additional requests so as to satisfy the DNS query of the client.

2. **Root nameserver:** The root nameserver is the first step in translating (resolving) human-readable hostnames into an IP address. A nameserver's operation is comparable to that of a library's index, which

points to various book racks and often serves as a pointer to other, more specialized locations.

3. **TLD nameserver:** It stands for the top-level domain server (TLD). It is comparable to a specific book rack in a library. The last portion of a hostname is hosted by this nameserver, which is the next step in looking for a specific IP address (In example.com, the TLD server is "com").

4. **Authoritative nameserver:** This ultimate nameserver resembles a dictionary on a bookshelf. A dictionary can be used to translate a specific name into its definition. In the nameserver query, this nameserver is the last stop. The IP address of the requested hostname will be returned to the DNS recursor (the librarian) if the authoritative name server has access to the requested record.

A Domain Name System (DNS) is concerned with a domain name being translated into the appropriate IP address for most situations. Understanding how this process works makes it easier to follow the course of a DNS lookup from a web browser to the DNS lookup process and back. Let's look at the steps one by one.

Note that DNS lookup results are frequently cached, either locally on the querying computer or remotely on the DNS infrastructure. A DNS lookup usually involves eight steps. When DNS information is cached, steps in the DNS lookup process are bypassed, making it faster.

Steps for Lookup in a DNS

- Let's say a user types "example.com" in a web browser. The query then travels through the Internet. It is received by a DNS recursive resolver.

- The resolver then further queries a DNS root nameserver.

- The root server would then respond to the resolver with a TLD DNS server (such as.com or.net), which would store the information for its domains. Our request is directed to the.com TLD when the user searches for example.com.

- The resolver then requests the .com TLD.

- The TLD server would then respond with the domain's nameserver's IP address, example.com.

- Finally, the recursive resolver queries the nameserver for the domain.

- The nameserver.

- Returns the IP address for example.com to the resolver.

- The DNS resolver then gives the web browser the IP address of the domain that was originally requested.

- The browser can request the web page when the eight steps of the DNS lookup have returned the IP address, for example.com.

- An HTTP request is sent to the IP address by the browser.

- The server at that IP returns the webpage to be viewed in the browser (step 10).

In reality, you also often enter "example.com/something" or anything like that. "example.com" is the domain, "/something" is the path. The domain and the path together make up the "URL" ("Uniform Resource Locator") of a website.

In addition to that, you can also visit most websites via "www.example .com" or just "example.com." Technically, "www" is a **subdomain**, but most websites simply redirect traffic from "www" to the main page.

Difference between Web Page/Website/WebServer/
Web Browser and Search Engine

- **Web Page:** A web page is a hypertext document displayed in any web browser like Chrome, Firefox, Safari, Edge, etc. A web page is also commonly referred to as a page.

- **Website:** A website is simply a collection of web pages. All of these web pages are interconnected and grouped so that the user can move from one page to another. It is often referred to as a site.

- **Web Server:** A web server is a computer used to host websites on the Internet. It is essentially computer software with suitable hardware used to accept requests via HTTP. A user initiates communication by making a request, and the server responds to it.

- **Web Browser:** A web browser, simply referred to as a browser, is application software used to access any type of content available on the world wide web. Anytime a user requests a specific web page or a particular website, the webserver retrieves the required content from the web-server, and then the browser displays that page on the user's screen.

- **Search Engine:** A search engine and a web browser are often con-fused, but they are different things. A search engine mainly helps you find other web pages by providing links to other websites. However, you need a web browser to access web pages through a search engine.

HTTP and HTTPS

What Is HTTP?

HTTP stands for Hypertext Transfer Protocol. It provides a set of rules and standards that regulate how any data on the web could be transferred. For web browsers and servers to interact, HTTP provides standard guidelines.

HTTP is a TCP-based application layer network protocol. It uses hypertext which is structured text that is used to establish the logical link between multiple nodes containing text. It is also called a "stateless pro-tocol" because each command is executed separately, without referencing the previous run command.

Advantages of HTTP

- HTTP can be implemented with other protocols on the Internet or even with other networks.

- HTTP pages are mainly stored on the computer and Internet caches which makes them quickly accessible.

- Platform independent which allows cross-platform porting.

- Does not need any Runtime support.

- Usable over Firewalls! Global applications are possible.

- Not connection-oriented; so no network overhead to create and maintain session state and information.

Disadvantages of HTTP

- There is no privacy, and anyone can see the content.

- Data integrity is also a huge issue as someone can alter the content. That's why HTTP protocol is insecure, as no methods for encryption are used.

- It is difficult to know the subject. Anyone can intercept the request and get the username and password.

What Is HTTPS?

Hypertext Transfer Protocol Secure is a highly advanced protocol. It is also a more secure version of HTTP. HTTPS uses port no. 443 for data communication purposes. It allows secure transactions by encrypting the entire communication with SSL. HTTPS uses a combination of SSL/TLS protocol and HTTP to provide an encrypted and secure identification of a network server.

HTTP allows you to create a secure encrypted connection between a server and the web browser of the client. It offers bi-directional security of data. Data is secure in both directions if it is coming or going. This helps in protecting potentially sensitive information from being misused or stolen.

In an HTTPS protocol, the SSL transactions are negotiated with the help of a key-based encryption algorithm. The key is usually either 40 or 128 bits in strength.

Advantages of HTTPS

- In most cases, the sites that are running over HTTPS will have some sort of redirect in place. This is why, even if you type in HTTP:// in the search bar, it will redirect you to HTTPS over a secured connection.

- It allows users to conduct safe e-commerce transactions, such as online banking, using this method.

- SSL technology protects all users and builds trust.

- An independent body verifies the certificate owner's identity. As a result, each SSL Certificate contains unique, verifiable information about its owner.

HTTPS's Limitations
The HTTPS

- The protocol is unable to prevent the theft of confidential information from browser cached pages.

- Only during network transmission can SSL data be encrypted. As a result, it is unable to delete the text from the browser's memory.

- HTTPS might increase the organization's computational as well as network overhead.

INTRODUCTION TO WEB DEVELOPMENT

It involves developing a website for the Internet or the World Wide Web. It is also used for Intranet (a private network) and Extranet. We have talked about Intranet and Extranet before. Web development has a varied range. It can go from developing a simple single static page of plain text to a complex web application that uses a special framework, electronic businesses, or social network services. Web development is a broad term that encompasses a wide range of activities such as web engineering, design, content development, client liaison, client-side scripting, server-side scripting, web server and network security configuration, e-commerce development, and so on.

In the circle of web professionals, web development mainly refers to the aspects of building websites that are not related to design, like writing markup and coding. It also entails the usage of content management systems (CMS) to make changes in the content easier and available with only a few basic technical skills.

For large organizations and businesses, web development teams consist of hundreds of people, and they follow standard methods like Agile methodologies in developing a website. Smaller businesses, on the other front, may only require a specific regular or contractual developer, as well as supplementary assignments to allied positions like graphic designers or information systems specialists. Web development is a collaborative effort between several departments rather than the domain of one designated department. There are primarily three kinds of Web developer specialization: frontend developer, backend developer, and full-stack developer. Frontend developers are responsible for behavior and visuals that run in the user browser, while backend developers deal with the servers.

From the time of commercialization of the web, web development has become a steadily growing industry. The growth of this industry relies on businesses, both big and small, wishing to use their website for advertising and selling products and services to customers.

There are many open-source tools for web development like BerkeleyDB, GlassFish, LAMP (Linux, Apache, MySQL, PHP), Stack, and Perl/Plack. Stacks like these have kept the cost of learning web development to a minimum. The rise of easy-to-use web-development software, such as BlueGriffon, Microsoft Visual Studio, and Adobe

Dreamweaver, have also played an important role in the expansion of the industry. Although knowledge of HTML or programming languages is required to use such applications, the fundamentals may be taught and implemented rapidly.

An ever-growing set of tools and technologies has helped developers build more dynamic and interactive websites. Further, web developers now help deliver applications as web services that were initially only available as applications on a desk-based computer. This has allowed for many opportunities when it comes to information and media distribution. One major example of this can be seen with the rise of cloud services with the likes of Adobe Creative Cloud, Dropbox, and Google Drive. These web services allow their users to interact with applications from various locations instead of being tied to one specific workplace for their application environment.

E-commerce brought a dramatic transformation in communication and commerce led by web development. Online auction sites such as eBay have also paved the way for consumers to find and purchase goods and services. Amazon or Flipakrt are some online retailers that have transformed many consumers' shopping and bargain-hunting experiences. One more example of transformative communication in the area of web development is the blog. There are various web applications such as WordPress and Movable Type that have created blog environments for individual websites. The usage of open-source CMS (content management systems) and enterprise content management systems have exponentially increased. This has extended web development's impact on the way we interact and communicate online.

Web development has also impacted the space of personal networking and marketing. Websites are no longer seen as simply tools for work or commerce but serve more broadly for communication and social networking. Users can communicate with organizations in a more personal and participatory way using social media platforms like Facebook and Twitter.

Many security flaws are considered throughout web construction, such as data entry error checking via forms, encryption, output filtering, and so on. Malicious techniques like SQL injection can be readily carried out by users with any ill intent but only a rudimentary understanding of web programming. Scripts can be easily used to exploit websites by granting unauthorized access to users with malicious intent that try to collect information such as email addresses, passwords, and sensitive content like debit cards and credit card numbers. Some of this is also dependent on the server environment on which the scripting language is running, such as ASP, JSP, PHP, Python, Perl, or Ruby, and therefore is not necessarily down to the web developer themselves to maintain. However, highly stringent testing of web applications with multiple test cases before a public release is heavily encouraged so as to prevent such exploits from happening. A captcha field must be included in any contact form on a website to prevent computer programs from automatically filling forms and sending spam.

Even after testing and launch, new security gaps are discovered in web applications, and security patch upgrades are routine for widely used programs. Web developers often have the job of keeping applications up to date as security patches are released, and new security concerns are discovered.

The various techniques used for keeping a web server safe from intrusion are called Server Port Hardening. There are many technologies that come into play when it comes to keeping information safe on the Internet when it is transmitted from one location to another. Like, for example, TLS certificates, also called SSL certificates, are issued by certificate authorities in order to help prevent Internet fraud. Many developers also employ different forms of encryption methods when transmitting and storing sensitive information. A basic understanding of information technology security concerns is often part of a Web developer's knowledge.

What Is Frontend Development?

Web development has two main parts, namely Frontend and Backend. Frontend development is also called client-side web development. In this book, we discussed frontend development in detail. It mainly entails creating web pages or web applications for the client using HTML, CSS, and JavaScript. Anything that appears on the client-side is something that the users can interact with.

Frontend development is a field that is constantly evolving. The tools and techniques keep on changing. The developer needs to always be ready to learn a new skill as the market is very volatile. With every new library or framework that comes out, the developer needs to upskill themselves. Awareness about how the market is developing is also important.

The objective of any developer behind designing a website is to make sure that whenever a user opens up a site, the information is arranged in such a format that the relevant information is easy to find. However, it becomes more difficult for the developer because there is now a wide range of devices with different screen sizes and resolutions available. The developer has to take these aspects into consideration so as to design a website suitable for every user. A website should render correctly for every browser (cross-browser), various operating systems (cross-platform), and different devices (cross-device).

In order to be a frontend developer, a person has to learn how to architect and develop websites and applications using web technologies. An Open Web Platform is used to operate these technologies. They can also act as compilation input for non-web-based platform environments like React Native. Anyone who enters the field of web development has to learn HTML, CSS, and JavaScript. These three technologies are deemed as the core.

Advantages of Frontend Development

- It provides quick development because of all the available modern frameworks and innovations. As the frontend is built quickly, the journey towards the final product also becomes shorter.

- It provides a secure coding environment. The entire set of code and the whole website is secure on any browser.

- Frameworks allow developers to create quick responding features that make the application work smooth and fast and respond well.

- The tools and techniques are easy to learn. Most of the frontend development is limited to the three core technologies that are HTML, CSS, and JavaScript.

- It provides robust features and a scalable environment.

Disadvantages of Frontend Development

- One of the biggest issues is code inflation. No matter how big or small a website is, customization is an essential part. In order to do that, the frameworks that are used for building the website indirectly led to a bigger codebase.

- Compared to the languages used at the backend like PHP and Java, which have been around for quite some time now, JavaScript is fairly new. Even though it is an essential component of the front end, the relatable and long-term knowledge is very limited.

- A newer version of frontend frameworks and libraries keep on releasing in quick succession. The continued fresh and major updates are more of a hassle as with the new versions, there is a bigger chance of messing up.

MAJOR CONCEPTS

The basic toolset is well defined: HTML, CSS, and JavaScript. However, the frontend development technologies may be extended with package managers, CSS preprocessors, frameworks, and many more.

HTML

The Hypertext Markup Language (HTML) is a standard markup language for displaying content in web browsers. It is mainly used to provide a structure to a web page so that content is aligned in a user-friendly way. This helps in viewing the document online in a browser.

As it is a markup language, it is made up of tags. Everything that is done in HTML is done with the help of tags. There are various tags that help in displaying text, ordered lists, unordered lists, tables, forms, etc. Any HTML document contains two main sections: head and body. Metadata which is used to describe the page is contained inside the head section. On the other hand, the body section includes all the tags that are used for representing visual content on any web page.

HTML is a completely platform-agnostic language. It works on all platforms, including Linux, Windows, and Mac. Web browsers receive the HTML pages from the webserver or from local storage. The documents received are then rendered into multimedia web pages. In HTML, the elements are the building blocks of any web page. Images, hyperlinks, interactive forms can also be embedded within a page.

There are multiple versions of HTML. The latest version is HTML 5. it has features like canvas, web socket, native audio, video support, geolocation, etc. HTML is an extremely simple language to use. Anyone can create an HTML file using a text editor and simply execute it in a browser.

The text between <html> and </html> contains the web page. The viewable content or body of the document is determined by the text between the opening and closing body tags.

<!DOCTYPE html> is added on the top and it is the Document Type Declaration for HTML5. It is included so that different browsers all render it in the same way and uniformity is maintained.

Since its release in 1991, HTML has been through many updates. HTML5 was publicly released for the first time in 2014. It has added features like offline media storage support, more precise content elements (i.e., header, footer, navigation), and audio and video embedding support.

Advantages

- It is widely used.

- It is supported by every browser.

- It is easy to learn and use.

- It is incredibly lightweight and loads fast.

- It is free.

- No need to purchase any extra software.

- It runs on any other browser or operating system.

- It has a loose syntax.

- Easy to write and code even for programming beginners.

- Allows for the utilization of templates which makes designing a web page easier.

- Useful for beginners who want to get into the web designing field.

- It is supported by each and every browser out there.

- HTML is built on every website.

- It is used for data storage like the XML syntax.

- It has various tags and attributes for different purposes, which shorten your time of coding.

Disadvantages

- It is a static language, so it cannot produce any dynamic output.

- Creating the structure of an HTML document is difficult.

- Even a small error can sometimes disrupt the whole flow of the web page.

- Creating an HTML web page from scratch is time consuming.

- It takes time to create a color scheme for any web page and to make lists, tables, and forms out of it.

- As it is a static language, you can only create plain and static pages with it.

- Just to make a simple web page, you'll need to write a lot of code.

- There are not many security features offered by HTML.

- As you need to write a lot of code, even for basic stuff, it creates some complexity.

- You need to check for deprecated tags and not use them. Other languages like CSS and JavaScript have taken over the functionality of that tag.

CSS

Cascading Style Sheets (CSS) is a style sheet language for describing an HTML document's style or appearance. CSS is considered as one of the core technologies for web development, primarily for frontend development. It provides web designers with control over how a website communicates with web browsers. It includes the formatting and display of the HTML documents.

It is a text-based coding language that is used to specify the website format. It defines the way a site could communicate with the web browser. By using CSS, web developers can regulate different style elements and functionalities.

CSS was designed by the World Wide Web Consortium (W3C). It was first released almost 25 years ago in December 1996. The latest version of CSS is CSS3. The .css file extension is used for CSS files.

CSS was specifically designed so that content of a web page and the styling of a web page could be kept separate. Separating the content and the presentation of a web page improves accessibility. It also helps in providing more flexibility and control over the presentation aspects of the web page.

The presentation of a web page includes the layout, fonts, colors, etc. Adding all the styles in a single style sheet allows us to use the same style sheet for designing multiple pages. This reduces the complexity and also helps in removing repetition from the structural content. The CSS file can be cached, which will increase the loading speed of the page when switching between pages that share the same formatting and styling.

CSS Frameworks
A CSS framework is a set of CSS and HTML files. It expands a frontend developer's website design skills. CSS frameworks not only aid in the creation of responsive designs but they also provide separate and symmetric layouts, saving developers from having to start from scratch every time. They are considered a good choice to fit diverse platforms and screen sizes. CSS frameworks considerably accelerate development workflow with common user interface components, grid systems, layouts, and many other features. Many frameworks exist in the CSS Universe:

- **Full-featured:** Bootstrap, Foundation, Semantic UI

- **Aimed at Material Design:** Materialize and Material Design Lite

- **Lightweight:** Pure

Sass and *Less* are two preprocessors. Short chores like finding up color values, closing tags, and other repetitive processes take a long time, whereas drafting CSS is routine. A preprocessor comes in handy in this situation. A CSS preprocessor is a scripting language for extending and assembling CSS.

The most popular preprocessors are Sass and Less. They share a few traits, such as:

- Backward compatibility with conventional CSS files and syntax elements

However, there are numerous distinctions between them.

- Syntactically awesome style sheets is what Sass stands for. Sass is a server-side scripting language that runs atop Ruby. The installation is offered via so-called gems (many Ruby/Rails libraries) due to its Ruby language origins.

- Leaner style sheets (Less). It's a JavaScript library that's rendered in the browser on the client-side. When combining JavaScript with style sheets, developers are significantly more likely to use Less. It's similar to writing ordinary CSS. The technology allows CSS to be reused within Less files.

Advantages

- Less complex, which reduces the collective effort required to style a web page considerably.

- Reduces the file transfer size.

- CSS provides the ability to reposition content. It helps in determining the changes within the position of web elements.

- By using CSS, a developer can easily specify a style for an element once and repeat it multiple times throughout the web page. It will automatically apply that required style.

- One style sheet can be reused across various websites and web pages.

- It simplifies the maintenance of code as you need to make the required changes only once in the style sheet, and it will reflect all across the website.

- It uses few lines of code, which increases the site speed.

- Less complex, so the effort is reduced.

- Helps in creating spontaneous and consistent changes.

- The changes made with CSS are device friendly.

- Helps in creating a responsive design with media queries so the websites can run smoothly on multiple devices.

- Easy to customize a web page.

- It helps in removing insignificant tags from the main page.

Disadvantages

- The CSS that works with one browser might not work properly for another browser.

- There are different versions of CSS, which might create confusion.

- In terms of security, CSS is not the best.

- Browser compatibility for different versions is dubious at best.

- There are multiple levels that are bound to create some confusion among new developers.

- CSS works differently in certain browsers like IE and Opera support CSS as a different logic.

- There might be some cross-browser issues.

- After making changes, we also need to confirm the compatibility.

DOM: The Web Page Structure

DOM stands for Document Object Model. The DOM is a cross-platform, language-independent interface that operates by constructing a tree structure from HTML content. Each tree node is an object that represents a section of the document. A document is represented as a logical tree in the Document Object Model. Each branch of the tree has a node at the end, and each node has an item.

DOM gives us programmatic access to a tree, which we may utilize to change the structure of the tree further. Changing the structure of the tree always entails changing the document's inherent behavior. The Document Object Model (DOM) is used to manipulate a page and change its behavior. Not only can the DOM be used to change the document's structure, but it can also be used to change the document's style and content. Attaching event handlers to nodes allows you to control the DOM. An event handler is called whenever an event is triggered.

W3C and WHATWG standards must be followed by the DOM. It works in the majority of browsers currently on the market. The DOM API is used to change the user interface with JavaScript. It accomplishes this by dynamically altering the HTML and CSS.

In real-world applications, DOM produces a document, such as an HTML page, by constructing a tree-like structure within the web browser. Every document's nodes are arranged in a tree structure. A DOM tree is the name for the tree structure. The "document object" node is at the very top of the tree.

Any browser that renders an HTML page downloads the HTML code into its local memory and then parses it automatically to show the page on the screen. The browser constructs a DOM of the page after it is loaded. The Document Object Model that was constructed would represent the HTML document in an object-oriented manner. It would then serve as a conduit between JavaScript and the document.

JavaScript

JavaScript is a text-based, interpreted programming or scripting language that allows us to implement complex features on any web page. JavaScript is incredibly lightweight and is mostly used for scripting web pages. It is also used to build web applications that interact with the client without reloading the page every time.

Most dynamic websites you encounter on the Internet employ at least some JavaScript. JavaScript is used whenever a website displays timely content updates, interactive maps, 2D or 3D graphics, a scrolling movie, or even a simple button that does something when you click on it.

Frameworks – These are templates that are used to create a website or a web application. They provide a structure to the project. The framework sets the page templates. Then it builds the structure in a particular allocated area. That area is used for embedding a framework code inside it.

So, JavaScript frameworks are complete sets of tools to form and arrange a website or web application.

Libraries – These are prewritten code snippets that can be used and reused in order to implement core features of JavaScript. The snippet can be easily integrated into any project code whenever deemed necessary.

So, libraries are basically specialized tools for particular coding needs, not an all-purpose machine for grooming the whole existing project.

Pros

- JavaScript always gets executed on the client-side regardless of where you host it. It saves lots of bandwidth and makes the execution process faster.

- XMLHttpRequest is an important object in JavaScript that was designed by Microsoft. The object call that is made by XMLHttpRequest is an asynchronous HTTP request made to the server. It helps in transferring data to both sides without reloading a page.

- One of the big advantages of JavaScript is that it has the ability to support all modern browsers. It also produces an equivalent result in every browser.

- JavaScript also receives support from the biggest companies in the world by creating projects. Like Google created Angular framework, in the same way, Facebook (now Meta) created the React.js framework.

- It is ubiquitous as it is used everywhere on the web.

- It works great with another language as well. Thus, it can be utilized in various types of applications.

- There are lots of open-source projects available that help the developer.

- Lots of community support and courses are available online to learn JavaScript easily and quickly.

- It allows creating rich interfaces.

- It is versatile, so you can create a whole JavaScript app from the front end to the back end using just JavaScript.

Cons

- It may be difficult to develop large applications solely on the basis of JavaScript. You might have to use the TypeScript overlay.

- It is applied to mostly large frontend projects. The configuration is tedious as the number of tools that are required to create an environment for such a project is a lot. That is why it is sometimes directly associated with the library's operation.

- The main disadvantage of JavaScript is that the code can be viewed by anyone.

- No matter how fast JavaScript interprets, the DOM (Document Object Model) is comparatively slow and can never render fast enough with HTML.

- If some error occurs in the JavaScript, then it can even stop the whole website. And this happens even though the browsers are extremely tolerant of errors in JavaScript.

- It is usually interpreted differently by different browsers. This makes it somewhat complex to read and write the browser code.

- Even though some HTML editors do provide the debugging feature, it is still not as efficient as other editors for languages like C and C++. This makes it tough for a developer to detect the underlying issue.

- The conversions take a longer time when converting a number to an integer. This not just increases the time needed to run the script but also reduces the overall speed.

SYNTAX AND CODE BASICS

HTML

HTML uses tags for its syntax. A tag is composed of special characters: <, > and /. They are interpreted by software to compose an HTML element. HTML elements usually come in pairs. There are two tags: opening tag and closing tag.

For opening an element with a start tag

1. , use <

2. then, the tag name (or element), without space

3. A tag ends with a >.

To close the simple element with an end tag

4. start it with </

5. then write the element name without space or (the tag name)

6. It usually ends with a >.

If the tag name is "blockquote," then you get

<blockquote> </blockquote>

Some elements do not need to have an end tag. Such elements are called empty elements.

For example, <br> and <hr>

br stands for a line break, and hr stands for horizontal rule

Attributes

An element can have attributes to refine its meaning.

The attributes are defined in the start tag itself. They consist of a name and a value, separated by an "=" character. Such as:

<tagname attribute="value"></tagname>

In HTML, the attribute value can remain unquoted if it doesn't contain spaces or any of the following characters: " ' ` = < or >. It has to be quoted using either (") single quotes or (" ") double-quotes. The value, with the "=" character, can be omitted if the value is an empty string.

Comments

If you write something in your code without disrupting how the browser will display your page, you can write **comments**. The browser will *ignore* them and are only useful for us humans who write the code.

A comment starts with <!-- and ends with -->.

CSS

Cascading Style Sheets (CSS) is a set of rules that contains three main parts – a selector, a property, and a value. The way CSS will run is based on two building blocks. These two blocks are properties and values. CSS runs as a combination of name-value pairs. Each property has its value.

- **Properties:** Properties are used as identifiers. These identifiers point to different characteristics like font, width, color, background color, etc. By using these properties, we can change the style of any HTML document.

- **Values:** Every property has multiple values that you can set. A value helps in altering the stylistic characteristics of a web page like the font size, width, background color, or the color of the text.

The property and value come together as a single pair and are collectively referred to as the CSS declaration. These declarations are placed inside a block of curly braces and are called CSS declaration blocks. Before getting deep into the theory, let us go through a basic example of a CSS block:

h3 { font size: 20px; line-height: 16px }

div { padding: 10px 10px 10px 40px }

p:hover, li { text-decoration: none }

In the above example, h3, p, and div are element selectors classes. In "heading 3," the font size is defined as 20 pixels and line-height as 16 pixels. Some padding is also given to the "div tag." The paragraph will be underlined when the user hovers on it.

Block Declaration in CSS

Declarations in CSS are separated into various blocks. Each declaration is wrapped within an opening curly brace "{ " and closing curly brace "}." Semicolons must be used to finish a declaration when it is contained within another declaration block; otherwise, the code will not operate or may provide unexpected results. A semicolon is not necessarily required for termination for the last declaration statement or block. However, it is a good practice to end with a semicolon so that we can prevent any unknown error from occurring.

Adding Comments in CSS

A CSS comment allows users to write something that isn't interpreted as a CSS command but still helps others understand how the code works. Most developers have experienced coming back to their code after a gap or interval of several months and not knowing what the code means. Moreover, these comments can also be helpful for temporarily remarking or noting out certain segments of your CSS code for testing purposes. In CSS, comments are written within /* and */.

In CSS, white spaces are used. White spaces are special characters that can be anything from a space to a tab to a new line. These white spaces are used to make a style sheet extra readable. Like HTML, the browser usually ignores almost all of the white spaces within your CSS code; and is meant to make the code human readable.

JavaScript

JavaScript syntax contains two types of values:

1. **Fixed values:** They are also called Literals.

2. **Variable values:** They are also called Variables.

JavaScript Fixed Values

The syntax rules for fixed values or literals are:

1. You can write numbers with or without a decimal.

2. Strings are written within single or double quotes.

JavaScript Variable Values

In any programming language, a variable is used to store data values.

In JavaScript, the keywords var, let, and const are used to declare the variables.

An equal sign is used for assigning values to variables.

JavaScript Operators

JavaScript uses arithmetic operators (+ - * /) to compute values and uses an assignment operator (=) to assign values to variables

JavaScript Expressions

An expression combines values, variables, and operators, which computes a value.

The computation is called an evaluation.

For example, 5 * 10 evaluates to 50

Expressions can also contain variable values.

JavaScript Keywords

They are used to identify tasks that must be completed.

They instructs the browser to create variables.

Additionally, the var keyword instructs the browser to create variables.

Comments in JavaScript

Not all JavaScript statements are meant to be executed.

The code that starts after double slashes // or between /* and */ is seen as a comment.

Comments are ignored and not executed.

Identifiers/Names

in JavaScript

JavaScript names are called identifiers.

Identifiers are used for the purpose of naming keywords, variables, and functions.

The rules for creating names that are legal are the same in most programming languages.

A JavaScript name must begin with:

- **A letter:** A-Z or a-z

- **A dollar sign:** $

- **An underscore:** _

The subsequent characters afterward may be letters, digits, underscores, or dollar signs.

JavaScript Is a Case-Sensitive Language

All JavaScript identifiers (keywords, variables, functions) are fully case-sensitive.

For example, let's consider two variables, lastName, and Lastname. These two are considered different variables.

CHAPTER SUMMARY

In this chapter, we learned about frontend development. We first learned how different aspects of the web work together. What is the Internet, and how does it work? All the different protocols and technologies involved make it work as smoothly as possible. Then we moved on to discuss what is frontend development and the core technologies that are used for it. And towards the end, we discussed the advantages and disadvantages of it. In the end, we talked about the syntax and the code basics of HTML, CSS, and JavaScript. We'll go over HTML 5 in depth in the upcoming chapter.

CHAPTER 2

HTML5

IN THIS CHAPTER

➢ Elements

➢ Design

➢ Attributes and tags

The previous chapter discussed frontend development and its advantages and disadvantages. We also learned about how the Internet and websites work in general. This chapter will discuss HTML5, which is one of the core technologies behind frontend development and its central concepts. We will learn about elements and design in HTML. We will also talk about attributes and tags in HTML.

ELEMENTS

HTML elements are components of Hypertext Markup Language (HTML) documents. HTML elements are used to add semantics and formatting to parts of a document like it is used to make text bold, organize it into paragraphs, lists, and tables, or embed hyperlinks and images. Other elements and text can be used as content for elements. HTML attributes can be applied to any HTML element. Attributes are used to give an element different properties. An HTML element can make use of some global attributes. Some properties, on the other hand, can only be applied to specified elements. Every attribute has a name and a value, and they are always in pairs. Attributes can only be specified in the start tag. We will

DOI: 10.1201/9781003309062-2

discuss more attributes in the later section. In this section, we will focus on HTML elements.

An HTML element contains a start tag, some content, and an end tag. The HTML element comprises everything from the start tag to the end tag.

Example - <tagname> Content </tagname>

There are also certain HTML elements that do not have any content or an end tag. Such elements are called empty elements.

Example - <hr> and

<hr> tag is used for horizontal line.

 tag is used for creating a line break.

HTML elements can also be nested within each other. Nested elements mean that one element can contain other elements within itself. Like the <body> element is nested in the <html> element. The element <html> is the root element and it is used to define the whole document. The <body> element is used to define the body of the document.

Note: An HTML element is composed of a start tag and an end tag and you should never skip the end tag even though some features will still display correctly even if you miss the end tag; however, it is strictly advised not to do so. Skipping the end tag could lead to unexpected results and errors.

Note: One other thing to keep in mind is that HTML tags are not case-sensitive. <BODY> and <body> would mean the same thing. Even though the HTML standard does not specify using lowercase, it is recommended to keep all your tags in lowercase. Using lowercase characters ensures uniformity as developers all across the globe use lowercase characters for writing HTML tags.

Their function for easier access has grouped each HTML element.

HTML5.

Root

\<html\>: The \<html\> element symbolizes the top-level element of any HTML document. It represents the root of the document and it is also referred to as the root element. The \<html\> tag serves as a container of all the other elements within a HTML document. Only the \<!DOCTYPE\> tag is contained outside of the \<html\> element. Also, there are certain attributes that you must declare for certain elements. The \<html\> tag always include the *lang* attribute. It is used in the start tag of the \<html\> element and it is used to declare the language of any web page. Declaring the language in which a web page is written makes it easier for search engines and browsers to categorize the page. The \<html\> tag also supports all the global attributes available in HTML.

Metadata

Metadata is referred to as the data that provides information about other data. In other words, metadata simply describes the kind of data we are dealing with without revealing the said data's actual content. The data could be a text message or an image, so the metadata could be that there is a string of text or an idea. It would not describe what the image is about or what the text says.

There are different types of metadata in real life as well as in HTML web-pages. In the context of HTML, metadata is something that contains information about the page. The data could range from the styles and the scripts used in the page to even data that would help the software in cataloging the web page. This software could be a search engine or a web browser, etc. The software would then use this data to learn how to render the page correctly for the user or the client. However, metadata related to the style and the script of the page could be defined on the same page or it could contain a link to another file. Mostly, it is linked to another file that has the information.

Some of the elements in HTML5 pertaining to metadata are:

\<base\>: the \<base\> HTML element is used to specify the base URL for the document. The base URL specified would then be used for all the relative URLs in a document. However, there can only be one \<base\> element within a document at any given point in time. The \<base\> tag should either have a href or a target attribute. It could also have both of them. The base element must be inside the \<head\> element.

<head>: the <head> element in HTML contains all the information that a machine can read or rather the metadata of the document. The <head> tag contains information like the title, script, character set, and style sheets. The head element is generally considered as the container for metadata. Metadata, as we discussed before, is data about data. In this case, it is data about the HTML document. Metadata is not displayed to the client. The <head> element is always embedded between the <html> tag and the <body> tag.

<link>: the <link> element in HTML specifies the relationship between the current document you are working on and an external resource. The external resource could be a style sheet, script, or even some favicon for your site. The most common use of link is for CSS style sheets. The <link> element is also an empty element. It only has a start tag that contains attributes. The attributes that can be included in the <link> tag are:

- **cross origin:** this attribute specifies how the element should handle cross-origin requests. The acceptable value for this attribute is *anonymous* and *use credentials.*

- **href:** this attribute is used to specify the location of the account that's been linked. The value for the href attribute is the *URL* of the document you wish to link.

- **hreflang:** this attribute is used to specify the language of the text in the linked document. The value for the hreflang attribute is *language_code.*

- **media:** this attribute is used to specify on which device the linked document should be displayed. The value for media attribute is *media_query.*

- **referrer-policy:** this attribute is used to specify which referrer should be used when fetching the resource. The acceptable values for this attribute are *no-referrer, no-referrer-when-downgrade, origin, origin-when-cross-origin, unsafe-*URL.

- **rel:** this attribute is used to specify the relationship between the current document and the document that's been linked. This attribute is required within the <link> tag. The values for the rel attribute are *alternate, author, DNS-prefetch, help, icon, license,* *next, pingback, preconnect, prefetch, preload, prerender, prev, search,* and *stylesheet.*

- **sizes:** this attribute is used to specify the size of the linked resource. However, this is only used of rel="icon". The value for this attribute is the height and width of the favicon.

- **title:** this attribute is used to specify the preferred or an alternate stylesheet.

- **type:** this attribute is used to specify the media type of the linked document. The acceptable value for this attribute is *media_type.*

<meta>: The <meta> element is used for defining metadata about an HTML document. The metadata that cannot be represented using other HTML elements (that are related to metadata) like base, link, style, title, and script are represented using the meta tag. Metadata is essentially data about data. <meta> tags are always nested inside the <head> element. They are mainly used to specify things like the character set, page description, document author, and viewport settings. Metadata is parsed by the machine and not displayed on the page. Metadata is used mainly by browsers, search engines, and other web services. The meta tag also lets developers take control of the viewport. Viewport is the small area of a web page visible to the users. The <meta> tag has attributes like charset, content, HTTP-equiv, and name.

<style>: The <style> element contains the information required to style a document. The style contains CSS. The CSS contained within the style element is then applied to the content of the document containing the style element. You can specify how HTML elements are rendered in a browser inside the style element. When a browser reads a style sheet it formats the HTML document according to the style information provided in the style sheet. If you have many style sheets linked in your document and numerous properties declared for the same selector or element in the separate style sheets, the value from the style sheet that is linked or read last by the browser will be utilized. In order to link an external style sheet, you need to use the <link> tag. The style tag also has attributes like media and type.

<title>: The <title> HTML element is used to define the title of the document. The title of a document is shown in the title bar of a browser or in the page tab. The title only contains text and the tags within the element are intentionally ignored. The title tag is necessary for all HTML documents. The title is significant when it comes to Search Engine Optimization (SEO). When listing pages to display after a search result, search engine algorithms use the page title to determine the order of the pages. The title element used for defining the title of a document is a browser toolbar. It also works as the title when you favorite or bookmark a page. It is also used as a title for the page in search engine results. In order to create a title that is also SEO friendly, go for a longer and more descriptive title. However, remember that search engines will only display about 50 to 60 characters of the title, so refrain from using titles longer than that. Most importantly, try to make your title relevant and meaningful in context to the content of the page. Do not use random descriptive words, as this will reduce the position of the page in search results. Also, you cannot have more than one <title> element in an HTML document.

Sectioning Root

<body>: The <body> HTML element is used to represent the content of an HTML document. Everything visible to the client is added to the <body> element, and there can only be one body element. The body element holds all of an HTML document's content, including headings, paragraphs, lists, images, hyperlinks, and so on.

Content Sectioning

Content sectioning elements are used for organizing the content of the document. The ingredients help in dividing the content into logical pieces. The sectioning elements are used for creating a broad outline of the page content. It includes both the header and the footer elements. Heading elements as well as elements used for navigation are also used for identifying and differentiating sections of content.

<address>: The <address> HTML element is used to indicate that the enclosed HTML is used for providing the contact information of a person or a group of people. This could also be used for organizations. This tag is primarily used to define the author's contact information or the owner of the document or the article. The contact information being provided could be an email address, a physical address, phone number, social media handles, personal website

URL, etc. The browsers render the text added within the address element in italic. The browsers also add a line break both before and after the address element.

<article>: The <article> HTML element is used to represent independent and self-contained content. An article should make perfect sense on its own and should be capable of being distributed independently from the site. The article element could be used in creating a forum post, a blog post, a magazine or newspaper article, an interactive widget, a product card, etc. It is important to know that using the article element is not going to render something special or different in the browser. You still need to use CSS to style the element and add desired effects.

<aside>: The <aside> HTML element is used to represent a portion of the content of an HTML document that is only loosely related to the document's main content. Asides are usually presented as sidebars or call-out boxes. It is important to know that using the aside element is not going to render something special or different in the browser. You still need to use CSS to style the element and add desired effects.

<footer>: The <footer> HTML element is used to define a footer for a document. It can also be used for a section for the nearest sectioning content or can be used for the sectioning root element. A <footer> mainly contains information about the author of the section, contact information, sitemap, copyright information, back-to-top links, or links to related documents. You can add several footer elements within a single document. Remember that if you add contact information inside the footer element, it should technically go inside an address tag.

<header>: The <header> HTML element is used as a container for introductory content, usually a set of introductory or navigational links. A header usually contains one or more heading elements (from h1 to h6), an icon or a logo, name and other information about the author, a search form, and various other elements. A single HTML document can have several header elements inside it. But it cannot be placed within another header element, address, or footer element.

<h1> to <h6>: The <h1> to <h6> HTML elements are used to define HTML headings. It represents six levels of section headings. <h1>

is the most important section heading whereas <h6> is the least important.

<main>: The <main> HTML element is used for creating the central content of the body of a document. The main content area has content that is directly related to the central topic of a document. It does not contain any type of content that gets repeated across all the documents. This includes navigation links, sidebar, site logos, copyright information, search forms, etc. There cannot be more than one element in a document. Also, the main element must not be a descendant of an element like header, nav, article, aside, etc.

<nav>: The <nav> HTML element is used to create a section of a page that provides navigation links. The main purpose of the nav tag is to define a set of navigation links. Those links could either be within the current document or could connect to other documents. Some common examples of navigation sections are indexes, menus, and tables of contents. However, it is not necessary for all links of a nav document to be inside a nav element. The nav element is only used for major navigational links. For people with disabilities, who use screen readers, browsers use the nav element to determine the initial rendering of the content.

<section>: The <section> HTML element is used to define a section of a document. A section element is more of a standalone element that does not have a more specific semantic element to represent it. Sections always have a heading and the exceptions are very few in that regard.

Text Content

The HTML text content elements are mainly used to organize blocks or sections of content. These elements are placed between the opening <body> and closing </body> tags. They are important from the standpoint of accessibility and SEO. These elements help in identifying the structure and purpose of that content.

<blockquote>: The <blockquote> HTML element is used to indicate that the text enclosed within is an extended quotation. Typically, it is rendered in a visual manner through indentation. A URL for the source site of the quotation can be given using the attribute cite. A textual representation of the source can also be given using the cite element. It primarily specifies a section that is quoted from some other source. For shorter and inline quotations, you can also use <q>.

<dd>: The <dd> HTML element is used for providing the description, definition, or value in a description list (dl). The dd element is also used in conjunction with the dt element. The dt tag is for defining certain names and terms. You can put images, line breaks, paragraphs, links, lists, etc. in add tag.

<div>: The <div> container for flow content is an HTML element. Unless and until the document is styled in any way using CSS, it has no influence on the content or layout. It can be easily styled using a class or an id. The div tag is also manipulated by JavaScript quite frequently. Styling is directly applied to the container. The div tag also works well with a layout model like Flexbox, which is applied to its parent element. It creates a division in an HTML document. The best part about div tag is that any content can be put inside it. Also, browsers provide a line break both before and after a div element.

<dl>: The <dl> HTML element is a description list. The element contains a list of terms that are specified using the dt element, and descriptions are provided by dd elements. The dl element is used in conjunction with both dd and dt tags. This element is commonly used to implement a glossary or to display metadata. This is done in the form of key-value pairs.

<dt>: The <dt> HTML element is used to define a term or a name in a description or definition list. It must be used inside a <dl> element. It is followed by a <dd> element. Multiple <dt> elements in a row are used to indicate several terms which are all defined by the immediate next dd element.

<figcaption>: The <figcaption> HTML element is used to define a caption or legend for a <figure> element. It describes the rest of the content of its parent element. It is usually placed as either the first or the last child of the figure element.

<figure>: The <figure> HTML element is used to specify self-contained content. It could be a diagram, photo, illustration, code listing, etc. with an optional caption. The caption is specified using the figcaption element. The figure, the caption, and the content are seen as a single unit. The content of the figure element is related to the main flow of the document, but the position however is independent. So, even if it gets removed, there is no effect on the flow of the document.

<hr>: The <hr> HTML element is used to show a break between two elements. It is displayed as a horizontal line separating the two tags or marking the end of one section and the beginning of the other.

<li>: The <li> HTML element is used to specify a list item. It must be contained inside an old or ul tag. <ol> stands for an ordered list and <ul> is for unordered list. In an unordered list, list items are displayed using bullet points. In ordered lists, they are displayed with a counter on the left. The counter could be a number or letter.

<ol>: The <ol> HTML element is used to define an ordered list. The list can begin with a number or an alphabet. The default is a numbered list. But you can change the value of the counter. A list can also further be styled by using CSS.

<p>: The <p> HTML element is used for a paragraph. Paragraphs are blocks of text that are separated from other blocks by blank lines. Browsers automatically add a blank line before and after a <p> element. It is a block-level element.

<pre>: The <pre> HTML element is used to represent preformatted text. The text within pre tag appears exactly as it is, which means all the spaces and line breaks are preserved. The text in pre tag usually gets rendered in the monospace font.

<ul>: The <ul> HTML element is used to represent an unordered list. It is usually rendered as a bullet list. The <ul> element is used in conjunction with the <li> tag to create an unordered list. For creating an ordered list, use <ol> tag.

Inline Text Semantics

The HTML inline text semantic elements are used to define the meaning. They also help create a structure by styling a word or a piece of text to stand out from the surrounding text.

<a>: The <a> HTML element is also called the anchor element. It is used to create a hyperlink with its href attribute, which specifies the link destination. It creates a hyperlink to web pages, files, email addresses, locations on the internet, or even on the same page. Without the href attribute, the <a> tag is just a placeholder for a hyperlink. The color scheme for links is that unvisited links are underlined and blue in color. A link that has been visited is under-lined and purple. An active link on the other hand, is underlined and red. If a user clicks on a link, it gets displayed in the same browser window unless and until a blank page is specified for the target/.

<abbr>: The <abbr> element in HTML represents an abbreviation or acronym; the title attribute can provide an expansion or descrip-tion for any abbreviation. If present, the title must contain the full description and nothing else.

<b>: The <b> element in HTML is used to draw the reader's attention to the element's contents, which are not otherwise granted. This was the old name for the Boldface element, and most browsers still render the text as boldface. While you should avoid using <b> to style text, the font-weight feature can be used to create boldface text, and the strong element can be used to indicate that text is extremely significant.

<bdi>: The <bdi> HTML element tells the browser bidirectional algo-rithm to treat the text it contains text. It's particularly useful when a website dynamically adds some text and doesn't know the direction-ality of the text being inserted.

<bdo>: The <bdo> HTML element overrides the current directional-ity of text, so that the text within is rendered in a different direction.

**
**: The
 HTML element produces a line break in text (car-riage-return). It is useful for writing an address or a poem where the division of lines is significant.

<cite>: The <cite> HTML element is used to describe a reference to a cited creative work that must include the title of that work. The refer-ence may be an abbreviated form according to appropriate conven-tions related to citation metadata.

<code>: The <code> element in HTML displays its contents styled to represent that the text is a short chunk of code. By default, the text is displayed using the agent default monospace font.

<data>: The <data> element in HTML links a given piece of content with a machine-readable translation. If the content is time or date related, the time element must be used.

<dfn>: The <dfn> element in HTML is used to indicate the term defined within the context of a definition phrase or sentence. The definition of the term is deemed to be the p element, the dt and dd pairing, and the section element, which is the closest ancestor of the <dfn>.

<em>: The <em> element in HTML marks text that has stress emphasis. The <em> can be nested, with each level indicating nesting to a greater degree of emphasis.

<i>: The HTML's <i> element specifies a region of text that is separated from the rest of the document for any purpose, such as text or technical jargon. Historically, these have been presented using italic type, which is the original source of the <i> naming of the element.

<kbd>: The <kbd> element in HTML represents a span of inline text representing textual user input from a keyboard, voice over input, or any other text entry device. Although the HTML standard does not require it, the agent defaults to rendering the contents of a <kbd> element using its default monospace typeface.

<mark>: Due to the marked passage's significance or importance in the enclosing context, the <mark> HTML element signifies material that is marked or highlighted for reference or notation reasons.

<q>: The <q> element in HTML indicates that the enclosed text is a short inline quotation. Most modern browsers implement this by surrounding the text in quotation marks. The element is intended for short quotations that don't require paragraph breaks; use the blockquote element for long quotations.

<rp>: The <rp> element in HTML is used to provide fallback parentheses for other browsers that do not support the display of ruby annotations using the ruby element. The <rp> element should enclose each of the opening and closing parentheses that wrap the rt element that contains the annotation's text.

<rt>: The <rt> element in HTML specifies the ruby text component of a ruby annotation, which is used to provide pronunciation, translation, transliteration information. The <rt> element must always be contained within a ruby element.

<ruby>: The <ruby> element in HTML represents small annotations rendered above, below, or next to base text, usually used to show the pronunciation. It can also be used for annotating kinds of text, but this usage is less common.

\<s>: The \<s> HTML element creates a strikethrough, or a line through, in text. To describe items that are no longer relevant or accurate, use the \<s> element. When indicating document edits, however, \<s> is not suitable; instead, use the del and ins components.

\<samp>: Inline text that represents sample (or quoted) output from a computer program is enclosed by the \<samp> HTML element. Its contents are usually displayed using the browser's monospaced default typeface (such as Courier or Lucida Console).

\<small>: Independent of its stylistic presentation, the \<small> HTML element conveys side comments and small print, such as copyright and legal material. It renders text within one font size smaller by default, such as small to x-small.

\<span>: The HTML element \<span> is a general inline container for expressing text that does not represent anything fundamentally. It can be used to group items for styling (using the class or id properties) or because they share attribute values, such as lang. It should only be used when no other semantic element is suitable. The span element is similar to the div element, except the div is a block-level element, whereas the span is an inline element.

\<strong>: The HTML element \<strong> denotes that the material is of high importance, seriousness, or urgency. The contents are usually displayed in bold type in browsers.

\<sub>: The \<sub> HTML element defines inline text that should be rendered as subscript for typographic purposes only. Subscripts are usually displayed with a lower baseline and smaller font.

\<sup>: The \<sup> element in HTML specifies inline text which is to be displayed as superscript for typographical reasons. These are usually rendered with a raised baseline using smaller text.

\<time>: The HTML element \<time> represents a specific time period. It might have the DateTime element, which converts dates into a machine-readable format, allowing for improved search engine results or custom functionality like reminders.

<u>: The <u> HTML element represents a span of inline text that should be rendered to indicate that it has a non-textual annotation. By default, this is rendered as a simple solid underline but may be altered using CSS.

<var>: The <var> element in HTML represents the name of a variable in a mathematical expression or a programming context. Although that behavior is browser dependent it's represented using an italicized version of the current typeface.

<wbr>: The <wbr> HTML element specifies a word break opportunity – a spot within the text where the browser can break a line even if its line-breaking rules would not otherwise break a line there.

Image and Multimedia

HTML5 supports different types of multimedia resources. Multimedia comes in different formats on the web, such as audio, video, animations, and images.

<area>: The <area> HTML element is used to define an area inside an image map with predefined clickable areas. An image map is primarily used to create geometric areas in an image that can be associated with a hyperlink. The <area> element is always nested inside a <map> tag. The usemap attribute in the tag <img> is linked with the *name* attribute of the <map> element. It is used to create a connection between the image and the map.

<audio>: The <audio> HTML element is used to embed any form of sound in a document. An HTML document could contain one or more than one audio sources. The audio is represented using the src attribute or even the source element. However, the browser will choose the more suitable one. You can also use this element for streaming media by using a MediaStream. Additionally, you can add text between the two audio tags. The text will only be displayed in the browser if the audio is not compatible with the browser. The audio formats supported by HTML are mp3, wav, and ogg.

<img>: The <img> HTML element is used to embed an image into the document. Images are linked to web pages rather than being physically put into them. The <img> tag creates a placeholder for the picture being referred.

The <img> has two required attributes:

1. **src:** it specifies the path to the image.

2. **alt:** If the image cannot be displayed for some reason, it offers an alternative text.

<map>: The HTML element <map> is used in conjunction with area elements to define an image map (a clickable link area).

<track>: The <track> HTML element is used as a child of the media elements, audio and video. It lets specific timed text tracks (or time-based data), for example, to automatically handle subtitles. The tracks are formatted in WebVTT format (.vtt files) — Web Video Text Tracks.

<video>: The <video> HTML element embeds a media player which supports video playback into the document. In your scripts, you can also substitute video for audio content, although the audio element may provide a better user experience.

Content

Embedded: HTML language can include a range of different content in addition to conventional multimedia content, even if it is not necessarily easy to interact with.

<embed>: The <embed> HTML element embeds external content at the specified point in the document. This content is given by an external application or any other source of interactive content such as a browser plug-in.

<iframe>: The <iframe> HTML element represents a nested browsing context, embedding another HTML page into the current one.

<object>: The HTML element <object> represents an external resource that can be regarded as an image, a nested browsing context, or a plugin-handled resource.

<param>: The <param> HTML element defines parameters for an object element.

<picture>: To provide alternate copies of an image for different display/device settings, the <picture> HTML element has zero or more source elements and one img element.

<portal>: The <portal> HTML element allows another HTML page to be embedded inside the current one for easier navigating between pages.

<source>: The <source> HTML element specifies multiple media resources for the picture, the audio element, or the video element. It is an empty element, which means that it has no content and doesn't have a (</>) closing tag. It is commonly used for the same media content in multiple file formats in order to provide compatibility with a wide range of browsers given their differing support for image file formats and media file formats.

SVG and MathML

You can embed format like SVG and MathML content directly into HTML documents, using the <svg> and <math> elements.

<svg>: The SVG element is a container that defines a new coordinate system and viewport. It is typically used as the document's outermost element, but it can also be used to embed an SVG fragment within an SVG or HTML document.

<math>: The top-level element in MathML is <math>. Every valid MathML attributes must be wrapped in <math> tags. In addition, you must not apply nested to a second <math> element in another, but you can have an arbitrary no. of other child elements in it.

Scripting

In order to create dynamic web applications and content, HTML supports the use of scripting languages, most prominently JavaScript. Certain elements support this capability.

<canvas>: Use the HTML <canvas> element with either the canvas scripting API or the WebGL API to draw graphics and animations.

<noscript>: If a script type on the website is unsupported or scripting is currently disabled in the browser, the <noscript> HTML element defines a block of HTML to be added.

<script>: The <script> HTML element is used to embed executable code or data; this is mostly used to embed or refer to JavaScript code.

The <script> element can be used with other languages, such as WebGL's GLSL shader programming language and JSON.

Demarcating Edits

These elements let others provide indications that specific parts of the text have been altered.

<del>: The <del> HTML element represents a range of text that has been deleted from a document. For example, it can be used when rendering "track changes" or source code different information. The <ins> element in HTML can be used for the vice versa purpose: To indicate the text added to the document.

<ins>: The <ins> HTML element represents a range of text that has been added to a document. You can also use the del element to similarly represent a range of text that has been deleted from the document.

Table Content

The elements used to create and handle tabular data.

<caption>: The <caption> HTML element specifies the caption (or title) of a table.

<col>: The <col> HTML element defines a column within a table and is used for defining semantics on all common cells. It is found within a colgroup element.

<colgroup>: The <colgroup> HTML element defines a group of columns within a table.

<table>: The HTML element <table> depicts tabular data, which is information presented in a two-dimensional table with rows and columns of data-filled cells.

<tbody>: The <tbody> HTML element encapsulates a set of table rows (tr elements), indicating that they comprise the body of the table.

<td>: The <td> HTML element defines a cell of a table that contains data. It participates in the *table model*.

<tfoot>: The <tfoot> HTML element defines a set of rows summarizing the columns of the table.

<th>: The <th> HTML element defines a cell as header of a group of table cells. The exact nature of the group is defined by the scope and header attributes.

<thead>: The <thead> HTML element defines a set of rows defining the head of the columns of the table.

<tr>: The <tr> HTML element defines a row of cells in a table. The row's cells can be established using a mix of <td> (means data cell) and <th> (means header cell) elements.

Forms

HTML encompasses a set of components that can be combined to construct questionnaires that users can complete and submit to a website or app.

<button>: The <button> HTML element represents a clickable button, used to submit forms or anywhere in a document for accessible, standard button functionality.

<datalist>: The option elements in the <datalist> HTML element represent the permissible or suggested options accessible to choose from within other controls.

<fieldset>: The <fieldset> HTML element is used to group several controls as well as labels (label) within a web form.

<form>: The <form> HTML element represents a document section containing interactive controls for submitting information.

<input>: The <input> element is used to create controls for web-based forms to accept user details, a wide variety of types of input data, and control widgets depending on the device and user agent. The <input> element is due to the vast quantity of input kinds and attributes, it is the most powerful and sophisticated in all of HTML.

<label>: The <label> HTML element represents a caption for an item in a user interface.

<legend>: The <legend> HTML element represents a caption for the content of its parent fieldset.

<meter>: The <meter> HTML element represents either a scalar value within a known range or a fractional value.

<optgroup>: The <optgroup> HTML element creates a grouping of options within a select element.

<option>: is used to specify an item within a select, optgroup, or datalist element. As a result, <option> can be used to represent popup menu items and other lists of things in an HTML text.

<output>: is a container element into which a site or app can inject the results of a calculation or the outcome of a user action.

<progress>: The <progress> HTML element displays an indicator showing the completion progress of a task, typically displayed as a progress bar.

<select>: The <select> HTML element represents a control that provides a menu of options.

<textarea>: The <textarea> element represents a multi-line plain-text editing control, useful to allow users to enter a sizable amount of form text, for example, a comment on a review or feedback form.

Interactive HTML Elements

These offer a selection of elements that help to create interactive user interface objects.

<details>: The <details> HTML element creates a disclosure widget in which the information is visible only when the widget is turned on means toggled into an "open" state. A label must be provided using the summary element.

<dialog>: The <dialog> HTML element represents a dialog box or other interactive component, such as a dismissible alert, inspector, or sub-window.

<menu>: The <menu> element is a semantic alternative to <ul>. It described an unordered list of items (described by <li> elements), each of these represent a common command or link that the user can activate.

<summary>: indicates a <summary>, <legend>, or <caption>, for a details element's disclosure box. Clicking the <summary> element toggles the state of the parent <details> element open and closed.

Web Components

They are an HTML-related technology that allows you to develop and utilize custom elements as if they were standard HTML elements. You can also make your own versions of basic HTML elements.

<slot>: part of the Web Components technology suite – is a placeholder inside a web component that you can fill with your own markup, which lets you create separate DOM trees and present them together.

<template>: The <template> HTML element is a mechanism for holding HTML that is not to be rendered immediately when a page is loaded but maybe instantiated subsequently during runtime using JavaScript.

Deprecated Elements

These are old HTML elements which are not be used. You should never use them in new projects and can replace them in old projects as soon as you can. They are listed here for the purpose of your understanding.

<acronym>: allows authors to clearly indicate a sequence of characters that compose an acronym or abbreviation for a word.

<applet>: embeds a Java applet into the document; this element has been deprecated in favor of the object.

<basefont>: The <basefont> element in HTML is deprecated. It sets a default font face, size, and color for the other elements which are descended from its parent element. Once set, the font size can then be varied relative to the base size using the font element.

<bgsound>: The <bgsound> element in HTML is deprecated. It sets up a sound file to play in the background when the page is being used.

<big>: The <big> deprecated element i HTML renders the enclosed text at a font size one level larger than the surrounding text. The size is capped at the browser's maximum permitted font size.

<blink>: The <blink> HTML element is a non-standard element which causes the enclosed text to flash slowly.

<center>: The <center> element in HTML is a block-level element that displays its block-level or inline contents horizontally centered within its containing element.

<content>: a part of the Web Components suite of technologies: was used inside shadow DOM as an insertion point and was not meant to be used in ordinary HTML. It has been replaced by the slot element, which creates a point in the DOM at which a shadow DOM can be inserted.

<dir>: The <dir> element in HTML is used as a container for a directory of files and/or folders, with styles and icons applied by the user agent. Do not use this element; instead, you should use the ul element for lists, including lists of files.

<font>: The <font> HTML element defines the font size, color, and face for its content.

<frame>: The <frame> element in HTML defines a particular area in which another document can be displayed. A-frame should use within a frameset.

<frameset>: The <frameset> HTML element is used to contain frame elements.

<hgroup>: The <hgroup> element in HTML represents a multi-level heading for a section of a document. It is a group a set of <h1>–<h6> elements.

<image>: The <image> HTML element is an ancient and poorly supported precursor to the img element. It should not be used.

<keygen>: to facilitate the generation of key material and submission of the public key as part of an HTML form. This mechanism is for use with web-based certificate management systems. It will be used in an HTML form along with other information required to develop a certificate request, and the result produced will be a signed certificate.

<marquee>: The <marquee> element in HTML is used to insert a scrolling area of text. You can also control what happens when the text reaches the boundaries of its content area using its attributes.

\<menuitem\>: The \<menuitem\> element in HTML represents a command that a user is able to invoke through a popup menu. The context menus and menus that might be attached to a menu button.

\<nobr\>: allows the text it contains from automatically wrapping across multiple lines, potentially resulting in the user having to scroll horizontally to see the entire width of the text.

\<noembed\>: The \<noembed\> HTML element is an obsolete, non-standard way to provide alternative, or "fallback," content for those browsers that do not support the element or do not support the type of embedded content. This element was cut off in HTML 4.01 and above in favor of a fallback content between the opening and closing tags of an object element.

\<noframes\>: permits content to be presented in browsers that don't support the frame element. However, the most commonly used browsers support frames. There are exceptions, including certain special-use browsers having some mobile browsers and text-mode browsers.

\<plaintext\>: The \<plaintext\> element in HTML renders everything following the start tag as raw text, ignoring any following HTML. There is no closing tag, till everything after it is considered raw text.

\<rb\>: It is used to delimit the base text component of a ruby annotation, i.e., the text that is being annotated. One \<rb\> element wraps each separate segment of the base text.

\<rtc\>: The \<rtc\> element in HTML embraces semantic annotations of characters presented in a ruby.The elements rb used inside of ruby element. rb elements can also have both pronunciation (rt) and semantic (rtc) annotations.

\<shadow\>: The \<shadow\> element in HTML. It is an obsolete part of the Web Components technology suite. It is used as a shadow DOM insertion point. You might use it if you have created multiple shadow roots under a shadow host. It is not useful in common HTML.

\<spacer\>: The \<spacer\> element in HTML is an obsolete element which allowed insertion of empty spaces on pages. It was designed by Netscape to accomplish the same effect as a single-pixel layout image, which web designers used to add white spaces to web pages without actually using an image. While <spacer> is no longer supported by any major browser, the same effects can now be achieved using simple CSS.

<strike>: The <strike> HTML element places a strikethrough (horizontal line) over text.

<tt>: The <tt> element HTML creates inline text which is presented as the user use default monospace font face. This element was created for the rendering text as it would be displayed on a fixed width display such as a text-only screen, or line printer.

<xmp>: The <xmp> element in HTML renders the text between the start and end tags without interpreting between and using a monospaced font. The HTML2 recommended that it should render wide enough to allow 80 characters per line.

DESIGN

HTML is a markup language that is basically used for structuring and presenting the content of a web page. To present the content in a way that makes it easier for the client to understand and interact with, HTML5 offers certain tags to create a layout. It represents the content in a way that is easier for the client to interact which requires a specific layout. As HTML was concerned only with structure before the content would be presented in a haphazard manner. The latest version of HTML solves that issue by encouraging developers to create a layout first. Using a predefined layout will eventually help the designers styling the web page through CSS. Using elements that they use for creating different sections of a web page, they can target and style a whole section in one go with CSS.

As we discussed above, HTML revolves around tags. Everything that you do in HTML is done with the help of tags. Tags are not displayed in the browser. The developers use them to create and label pieces of content and design them accordingly. There are lots of tags which are used commonly within the body tag to display content. The most common tags are the heading tags (from h1 to h6), paragraph tags, list tags (ordered and unordered tags), anchor tags (used for linking), and div tags (used for dividing blocks of content).

The heading tags are used for organizing the content. The six heading tags available are from <h1> to <h6>. Each of these heading tags has its own opening and closing tags. The heading structure in an HTML document can be seen as a pyramid structure with the biggest tag <h1> on top of the pyramid whereas the smallest one <h6> is at the bottom. <h1> is the biggest heading, so it is also seen as the one for displaying the most important content. <h2> and <h3> are used for adding the supporting details. It is used mainly as a sub-heading. <h4> and <h5> are generally used for representing the sidebar details. The least important heading is represented using the <h6> tag. The heading at the top (h1 tag) is used the least, and as you go down the level, the headings are used more and more depending on the content.

The paragraph tags (<p> and </p>) are mainly used for containing paragraphs. Most of the time, any content that is not a heading or a bullet list is considered a paragraph and put inside the <p> tags. However, paragraph tags should mainly be used for representing the main content area of a website. You can also use them in different places/locations. But for the sake of clarity and overall document organization, it is better to keep the tags limited to the main content area.

The list tags encompass two types of lists: ordered lists and unordered lists. Ordered lists consist of a list starting with numbers, alphabets, or even roman numerals. Unordered list consists of a list with bullet points. An ordered list is represented using the <ol> tag and an unordered list is represented using the <ul> tag. The opening and closing <ul> and <ol> tags represent the starting and stopping points of the list. Now both ordered and unordered lists use <li> for representing a list item. All the items that are part of the list are represented using the <li> tags. The list item's content is encompassed inside an opening and closing <li> tag.

The anchor tags are used to create links. These links could be across the website itself or outside the website. The anchor tags are mainly used for creating anything clickable. The anchor tag needs an opening and closing tag to function like any other HTML element, but it also needs an attribute href for adding the link. If you wish to direct the user to a URL, use the href tag. If you wish to add text that would be displayed within the hyperlink then add text within the anchor tag. The text added is also called anchor text. The basic format for an anchor tag is shown below.

<a href = "www.something.com"> Anchor Text/ Text you want to make a clickable link </a>

The above text would get displayed like this: Anchor Text/ Text you want to make a clickable link

There are also other ways to make an element clickable, but they require the usage of some complex concepts and use JavaScript to do that which is out of scope for this lesson.

The div tag is possibly the most versatile tag in HTML. The div tag doesn't have its own usage per se, but it has the ability to be modified and used in any form that the developer deems suitable. The div tag is a simple tag that is used as a container surrounding other elements of the page. The div element act as a container for the page's numerous elements. Creating a block of containers with div that contains many elements makes it easier to style, organize, and divide the documents. Using a div tag we can group several elements together and style them in a collective manner using CSS style for the entire group.

HTML Layout Elements

Websites usually display content in multiple columns across the web page. Content placement within a web page is somewhat similar to a magazine or newspaper. There are some special elements in HTML that help us in creating our layout. These elements are:

- **<header>**: Used to define a header for a document or a section.

- **<nav>**: Used to create a navigation bar and set navigation links for the navbar.

- **<section>**: Used to define a section within a HTML document.

- **<article>**: Used to define independent content or used as a container for an article.

- **<aside>**: Used to define content aside from the main content, mainly towards one side of the page. Works in a similar fashion as the sidebar.

- **<footer>**: Used to define a footer for a document or a section.

- **<details>**: Used to insert additional details into the web page that the user can open or close on demand.

- **<summary>**: Used to define a heading for the <details> element.

These layout elements are also called semantic elements, and they are used to define different parts of a web page. We will discuss semantic elements in detail and learn more about document and website structure using HTML in a while.

HTML Layout Techniques

There are different techniques available for creating layouts. However, each of them has its own set of advantages as well as disadvantages. It depends on the developer and how they choose what works best for them. Now, we will discuss some of the techniques with which we can create layouts.

- **Frameworks:** For creating a layout quickly and easily, there is no better option than using a framework. There are loads of CSS frameworks available in the market like Bootstrap, Foundation, etc.

- **Float property:** The CSS float property is powerful enough that you can create the entire layout of a web page using it. The CSS float property is also very easy to learn. However, the issue with using float is that the floating elements depend on the document's flow. In case the flow of the document gets disrupted by something like the screen resolution, then the content placement will look haphazard. Using the float layout is not a suitable option, especially when creating a responsive website.

- **Flexbox:** Using the flexbox model to design the layout of a web page ensures that the elements behave in a predictable manner. Even when the screen resolution changes, the content should align itself in such a way that it is easy for the client to understand. A flexbox works great when it comes to accommodating different types of screen sizes and different types of display devices.

- **Grid:** Using the grid layout model makes it easier to design web pages without having to use floats and positioning. The grid model is a grid-based layout system that uses rows and columns.

HTML Responsive Web Design

A responsive web design is the kind of design that automatically adjusts to the different screen sizes and viewports. Creating a responsive design is very important so that your website looks great on all devices. When you create a responsive web design using HTML and CSS, the website must be able to automatically resize, shrink, hide, or enlarge the website according to the screen resolution and the device of the user. The website should be accessible from all types of devices like desktops, tablets, and mobile phones.

In order to create a responsive design, you need to first set a viewport. To add a viewport, add the meta tag within your head tag.

<meta name = "viewport" , initial-scale = 1.0" content = "width = device-width>

Adding the meta tag as shown above will set the viewport of your page. Viewport is added to give the browser instructions on how to control the dimensions of a page and how to scale it according to the devices it encounters.

Responsive design.

In the same way, we can also make the images on our web page responsive. Responsive images enhance the website as they would scale to fit any browser size. You can set the CSS width property to 100%; this will make the image responsive and scale it up and down accordingly. However, if you use the width property, the image will scale more than its original size if it encounters a bigger screen. A simple solution to this would be using max-width property instead of width property. Using max-width property at 100% ensures that the image will scale down accordingly, but it would never scale up to be bigger than its actual size.

You can also show different images based on the browser width. The <picture> element in HTML allows you to do that. By using this element, you can define different images for different browser window sizes. You can check if it is working correctly by resizing the browser window.

In order to make the text responsive, you can use the unit VW, which stands for viewport width. Using VW as a unit will ensure that the text size will follow the browser window's size. The new unit works by calculating the viewport of the screen. Viewport is the actual size of the browser window. So, if you put the value as 1 vw, it will be equivalent to 1% of the width of the viewport. If the viewport is 50 cm wide then 1 vw would be equal to 0.5 cm.

Media queries are one of the most common approaches to make a website responsive. Using media queries makes it possible to create completely different styles based on different browser sizes. A responsive web page will look regardless of the fact that it is opened on a desktop or a mobile phone. If you use a CSS-based framework then it will offer responsive design. You can create a responsive web page without using various methods like adding media queries, making images responsive, etc.

Semantic Elements

It is an element with a meaning. A semantic element clearly describes its meaning and purpose to both the browser and the developer. On the other hand, non-semantic elements say nothing about the content they contain within themself. <div> and <span> are non-semantic elements that are used quite frequently. Semantic element clearly defines its content so elements like <form>, <table>, and <article> are few examples of it. Let's look at the common examples of semantic elements used for creating a website structure.

<section>: Used to define a section in a document. According to the official documentation by W3C, a section is considered a thematic group of content, typically with a heading. A web page is usually split into different sections like introduction, content, contact info, etc.

<article>: The article element is used to specify independent and self-contained content. A defining factor of an article is that it should make sense on its own, independent of the website content surrounding it. An article content should also be possible to get distributed independently than the rest of the website. The <article> element can be used in blog posts, user comments, forum posts, product cards, newspaper articles, etc.

<header>: The header element is used as a container for introductory content or a set of navigational links. A header element can contain one or more heating elements, a logo or an icon, and information about the admin or the author. Even though you can have several header elements within one HTML document you cannot place a header within a <footer> tag, an <address> tag, or another <header> element.

<footer>: Define a footer for a document or a section. The footer element mainly contains copyright information, contact information, sitemap, authorship information, back-to-top links, etc. You can also have several <footer> elements within one document.

<nav>: The nav element is used to define a set of navigation links. The nav element contains the main navigation links for the web page. People with disabilities who use screen readers use this element to determine where to omit the initial rendering of this type of content.

<aside>: Define content aside from the main content placed in the center. It can be seen as something similar to a sidebar. However, the aside content should be indirectly related to the content surrounding it.

<figure> and <figcaption>: Both these elements are used in tandem with each other. The figure tag specifies self-contained content like photos, diagrams, illustrations, code listings, etc. On the other hand, the figcaption element is used to define a caption for the figure element. The figcaption element can be placed either as the first or the last child of a figure element. The <img> element is used for adding an image or illustration.

Creating a Website Structure

HTML has a number of block levels used to define a website's areas. The areas could be the header, the navigation menu, the main content column, etc. Web pages usually look different from each other when it comes to the visual aspects of a website, but all of them tend to share some similar standard components. The main components are as follows:

- **Header:** The header is identified as a big strip on top of any web page with a big heading, logo, and perhaps even a tagline. This feature usually stays the same from one webpage to another.

- **Navigation Bar:** The navigation bar is used to link to the site's main sections, and it is usually represented by menu buttons, links, or tabs. Just like the header, the navigation bar remains the same from one web page to another. Having a consistent navbar is also an important consideration when it comes to a satisfactory user experience. An inconsistent navbar will leave the users confused and unsatisfied.

Many web designers consider the navigation bar to be a part of the header rather than seeing it as an individual component. However, it is more of a personal choice rather than a requirement. Some people even go on to say that having these components as separate is better for accessibility. Separating the header and the navigation bar allows screen readers to read the two features better.

- **Main Content:** The unique content of any web page is displayed at the center of the page, considered as the main area. The main content area is a must in every website; however, the actual content in the main area is bound to differ from website to website.

- **Sidebar:** The sidebar contains peripheral information like links, quotes, ads, etc. The content in the sidebar depends on the main content. The sidebar content is usually related to the main content. In some websites, the sidebar also contains a secondary navigation system. Like in a blog website, the sidebar could contain the links to previous articles, the author's social media profile links, etc.

- **Footer:** Just like the header, the footer is a strip across the bottom of the page. The footer usually contains fine print, copyright notices, or contact information. The footer is also used to provide common information, but mostly the information in the footer is secondary when it comes to information in the header. The footer is also used for SEO purposes at times. It provides direct access links to popular content.

For increased ease of access for visually impaired people, it is important to mark up sections of content based on their functionality in the HTML code. You can use elements of content that describe the sections above. Screen readers can recognize these elements and can prove to be of great help for people with visual disabilities. To implement such a structure and layout, HTML provides tags that are named as semantic elements. You can use these semantic elements to represent such sections.

- **Header**: use <header> tag

- **Navigation Bar:** use <nav> tag

- **Main Content:** use <main> tag and add nest other elements like <article>, <section>, and <div> tag inside it.

- **Sidebar:** use <aside> tag which is often placed inside <main> tag.

- **Footer:** use <footer> tag

Non-semantic Elements

It is hard to find a semantic element that would be ideal to group some items together or wrap some content in some situations. Other times, you might want to group a set of elements together so they can be classified as a single entity. For such cases, you can use the <div> or the <span> tag. You should use these with a class attribute to style all the elements within div and span collectively.

Span is an inline non-semantic element. You should mainly avoid using span. You should only use it in case you cannot think of a better text element to wrap around your content. Or if you don't want to add any meaning.

Div on the other hand is a block-level non-semantic element. Only use a div tag if you cannot think of a better semantic block to use or you do not want to add any specific meaning.

ATTRIBUTES

Attributes are used to provide additional information about HTML elements. All HTML elements can have attributes because there are some global attributes that work with all elements. Attributes are specified as the starting tag and they come in name-value pairs. The name of the attribute would equate to the value of the attribute. Attributes are essentially used to configure the elements or adjust their behavior to meet the user criteria. Let's take a look at all the attributes available and what they are used for.

- **accept:** used with the element <input>. The accept parameter is being used to indicate what file types a server will allow. The file should be submitted through a file upload. The accept attribute takes its value as a list of commas separated by one or more file types. In previous versions of HTML accept attribute, the <form> element was also used.

- **accept-charset:** used with the element <form>. When submitting a form, the accept-charset parameter is used to indicate the character encoding.

- **accesskey:** this is a global attribute and specifies a shortcut to activate or focus on an element.

- **action:** used with the element <form>. It specifies where the data would be sent after submitting a form. It essentially processes the information submitted via a form.

- **align:** this attribute with multiple elements like <applet>, <caption>, <col>, <colgroup>, <hr>, <iframe>, <img>, <table>, <tbody>, <td>, <tfoot>, <th>, <thead>, <tr>. It specifies the horizontal alignment of any element in reference to the surrounding elements. This attribute is no longer supported in HTML5, so you need to use CSS instead.

- **allow:** it is used with the element <iframe>, and it helps in specifying a feature policy for the iframe.

- **alt:** it can be used with the elements <area>, <img>, and <input>. The alt attribute is used to provide alternative information about an image. This one is implemented so if a customer can't see the display for some reasons, such as a connectivity issue, a src tag problem, or using a screen reader, they may still understand what the picture is all about. You can also create a tooltip using the title attribute. Using an alt attribute is required when using the img tag. In case of input element, the alt attribute can only be used if the type attribute is equal to the image.

- **async:** this attribute goes with the script tag and is used for executing the script asynchronously. It is a boolean instance which means it accepts values only in true and false. In case the value is true, the script gets executed asynchronously as soon as it is available. It is mandatory to note that this feature is used only for external scripts and it should only be used if the src feature is already present. There are multiple ways to execute an external script.

  1. If async is present, the script gets executed asynchronously like the rest of the page. The script gets executed while the page continues on with the parsing.

  2. If defer is present and async is not present, then the script would be executed after the page finishes its parsing.

  3. If neither async nor defer is present, then the script gets fetched and executed immediately, even before the browser continues parsing the page.

- **autocapitalize:** it is a global attribute. This attribute capitalizes the input set by the user automatically.

- **autocomplete:** used with elements like <form> and <input>. This attribute specifies whether the controls of the form can have their values automatically completed by the browser or not. A form or input field can turn the autocomplete on or off. It helps the browser to predict the value. Whenever a user types in a field, the browser would start displaying options based on the values typed earlier. It is not necessary to have the autocomplete option on for both form and input. You can turn autocomplete on for form and off for input and vice versa. The autocomplete attribute works with certain input types like text, search, URL, email, tel, range, color, password, date pickers, etc.

- **autofocus:** this attribute is used with elements like button, input, select, and textarea. The autofocus attribute automatically focuses on something right after the page is loaded. It is a boolean attribute. When it is present, it automatically lays focus on that element.

- **autoplay:** this attribute is used with elements like audio and video. It is a boolean attribute and specifies that the audio or video should play as soon as possible. If the value is true, the audio/video would start playing automatically as soon as possible and without stopping.

- **background:** this attribute is used with elements like <td>, <th>, <body>, and <table>. It is used for specifying the URL of any image-based file. Even though this attribute is still supported by lots of email clients and browsers, it is still obsolete. So, refrain from using it and use CSS background-image property instead.

- **bgcolor:** this attribute is used with elements like body, col, colgroup, marquee, table, tbody, tfoot, td, th, tr. It sets the background color of any element. As it is a legacy attribute, you should use the background color property of CSS instead.

- **border:** this attribute is used with elements img, object, and table. It is used to specify the width of the border of any element. As it is a legacy attribute, you should use the border property of CSS instead.

- **buffered:** this attribute is for audio and video elements, and it contains the time range of an already buffered media.

- **capture:** this attribute is used with the element input. It specifies if a new file can be captured or not from the media capture specification.

- **challenge:** this attribute is used with the element keygen. In this a challenge key gets submitted along with a public key.

- **charset:** this attribute is used with the element meta and script. When used with the element meta, it is used to specify the character encoding for the HTML document. However, when the charset attribute is used with the script element, it specifies the character encoding used in any external script file. The usage of UTF-8 character set is encouraged by HTML5 specification as it contains almost all the characters and symbols in the world.

- **checked:** this attribute is used with the element command and input. It indicates if an element should be checked on page load or not.

- **cite:** this attribute is used with the element blockquote, del, ins, and q. the value contains a URL that redirects to the source of the quote being cited.

- **class:** it is a global attribute which means it can be used with any element. Most often, it is used to style elements with the help of CSS properties.

- **code:** this attribute is used with the element applet. It specifies the URL of the file that is to be loaded and executed.

- **codebase:** this attribute is used with the element applet. It specifies the absolute or relative URL of the directory.

- **color:** this attribute is used with the element basefont, font, and hr. It is used to set the text color either by using the hexadecimal format (#RRGGBB) or by specifying the name. The color attribute is no longer used and is considered a legacy now. Instead, the CSS color property is used in its place.

- **cols:** this attribute is used with the element textarea. It defines the number of columns that can be displayed in a textarea.

- **colspan:** this attribute is used with the element td and th and it represents the number of columns a particular cell should span.

- **content:** this attribute is used with the element meta. It is basically a value that is associated with name or HTTP-equiv depending on the context in which the tag is used.

- **contenteditable:** it is a global attribute which means it can be used with all the elements. It specifies when the content of an element is editable or not.

- **contextmenu:** this is also a global attribute. It is used to define the ID of any menu element, which eventually ends up serving as the element's context menu.

- **controls:** this attribute is used with the element audio and video. It specifies whether a browser should show playback controls to the user or not.

- **coords:** this attribute is used with the element area. It indicates a set of values that specify the coordinates of a hotspot region.

- **crossorigin:** this attribute is used with elements like audio, video, script, link, and img. It defines how any element should handle cross-origin requests.

- **CSP:** this attribute is used with the element iframe. It specifies the Content Security Policy. Any document that is embedded must agree to enforce it.

- **data:** this attribute is used with the element object. It indicates the URL of any resource.

- **data-*:** it is a global attribute that lets you attach custom attributes to any HTML element.

- **DateTime:** this attribute is used with the element-time, del, and ins. It specifies the date and time associated with any element.

- **decoding:** this attribute is used with the element img. It specifies the preferred method to decode an image.

- **default:** this attribute is used with the element track. It specifies whether the track should be enabled or not. It switches accordingly depending upon the user's preferences.

- **defer:** this attribute is used with the element script. It gets executed by the browser engine after the page has been parsed.

- **dir:** it is a global attribute. This feature is used to indicate the text direction. The allowed values are LTR (Left to Right) and RTL (Right to Left)

- **dirname:** this attribute is used with the element input and textarea.

- **disabled:** this attribute is used with the element button, command, fieldset, keygen, input, optgroup, select, option, and textarea. It specifies whether a user can interact with an element or not.

- **download:** this attribute is used with the element a and area. It is used to indicate that a particular link is to be used for downloading a resource.

- **draggable:** it is a global attribute. It specifies if an element is draggable or not.

- **enctype:** this attribute is used with the element form. When the method is POST, this attribute is used to specify the content type of the form data.

- **enterkeyhint:** this attribute is used with the element textarea and contenteditable. It describes which action label or icon to be displayed in place of enter key on virtual keyboards. It can also be used with elements in an editing host like contenteditable attribute. In the same way, it can be used with form controls like textarea elements to set its values.

- **for:** this attribute is used with the element label and output. It specifies the elements that belong to this one.

- **form:** this attribute is used with elements like input, fieldset, button, label, meter, object, keygen, output, select, textarea, and progress. It simply specifies the form which is the owner of that element.

- **formaction:** this attribute is used with the element button and input. It specifies the action of any element. This attribute is primarily used to override the action that has been defined in the form.

- **formenctype:** this attribute is used with the element button and input. If type = "submit" is used for either button or input, the attribute would set the corresponding encoding type during form submission. This attribute would override the enctype attribute that specifies the button's form owner if specified.

- **form method:** this attribute is used with the element button and input. This sets the submission method to use during form submission in case type = "submit" is specified for button/input. There are various submission methods like GET, POST, etc. It also overrides the specified method attribute of a button's form owner.

- **formnovalidate:** this attribute is used with the element button and input. A boolean attribute states that the form should not be validated when it is submitted. Upon specifying this attribute, the novalidate attribute gets overridden.

- **formtarget:** this attribute is used with the element button and input. It states the browsing context that should be used to display the response received after submitting a form. The response could be displayed in an inline frame, tab, window, etc. This attribute can also override the target attribute of the form owner of a button.

- **headers:** this attribute is used with the element td and th. This indicates the IDs of the elements relevant to the element.

- **height:** this attribute is used with the element iframe, embed, canvas, input, img, object, and video. It states the height of all the elements mentioned. In order to set the height of other elements, you need to use the CSS height property. Even for certain elements like div, it works as a legacy attribute.

- **hidden:** this is a global attribute that helps in preventing the rendering of any element. Although it keeps the child elements like script active at the same time.

- **high:** this attribute is used with the element meter. This helps in defining the lower bound of an upper range.

- **href:** this attribute is used with the element a, link, base, and area. It helps in adding the URL of the resource that you want to create a link of.

- **hreflang:** this attribute is used with the element a, area, and link. It states the language of a hyperlinked resource.

- **HTTP-equiv:** this attribute is used with the element meta. It is used to indicate a pragma directive.

- **icon:** this attribute is used with the element command. It shows the picture that represents the command.

- **id:** this is a global attribute that is used in conjunction with CSS. It is primarily used to style a specific element and it overrides the styling provided by the class attribute. The value of this attribute has to be unique as it is used to create a custom style for an element.

- **importance:** this attribute is used with the element iframe, img, link, and script. It usually specifies the relative fetch priority of any resource.

- **integrity:** This attribute is used with the element script and link. It indicates a subresource integrity value that is used by browsers for verifying what they are fetching.

- **intrinsicsize:** this attribute is used with the element img. It tells the browser to ignore the intrinsic size of an image and pretend that the size specified through the attribute is the actual size.

- **input mode:** this attribute is used with the element textarea and contenteditable. It mainly provides an inkling about the type of data that might get entered by the user while they are editing an element or the contents of it. The input mode attribute can either be used with form controls or in elements that require an editing host. The form controls can be used to set values of textarea elements whereas contenteditable attribute can be used with elements in an editing host.

- **ismap:** this attribute is used with the element img. It specifies that the image is actually a part of a server-side image map.

- **itemprop:** this is a global attribute and can be used to add properties to an item. It consists of a name-value pair. Each name-value pair is referred to as a property.

- **keytype:** this attribute is used with the element keygen. It indicates the type of key that is generated.

- **kind:** this attribute is used with the element track. It indicates the type of the text track.

- **label:** this attribute is used with the element option, track, and optgroup. It shows a user-readable title of an element.

- **lang:** this is a global attribute. It states the language that is used in an element.

- **language:** this attribute is used with the element script. The use of this attribute has been deprecated since. Previously, this was used for defining the script language used in the element.

- **loading:** this attribute is used with the element img and iframe. This is used for specifying the loading state of an element. Either the element gets loaded lazily or immediately. The specified value for each of these states is loading = "lazy" or loading = "eager" simultaneously.

- **list:** this attribute is used with the element input and it creates a list of predefined options to suggest to the user.

- **loop:** this attribute is used with the element audio, video, marquee, and bgsound. It specifies whether a video should start playing back again from the start after it is finished.

- **low:** this attribute is used with the element meter. It shows the upper bound of the lower range.

- **manifest:** this attribute is used with the element HTML. It specifies the URL of the document's cache manifest. The manifest attribute has been deprecated now and in order to use the same functionality rel = "manifest" is used within the link element.

- **max**

- **maxlength**

- **minlength**

- **media**

- **method**

- **min**

- **multiple**

- **muted**

- **name**

- **novalidate**

CHAPTER SUMMARY

In this chapter, we learned about HTML5 and how it works. We also learned about the different elements, attributes, and tags used in the markup. In the next chapter, we will go through CSS3 and see how it works.

CSS3

IN THIS CHAPTER

➤ What is CSS?

➤ What is new in CSS3

➤ CSS preprocessors

In the previous chapter, we talked about HTML 5. We discussed all the different elements available in HTML. We also talked about how we can create layouts and design using HTML. We also learned how the different attributes work and for what purpose each of them is used. This chapter will learn about CSS3 which is one of the core technologies behind frontend development. We will talk about CSS and its major concepts. We will learn about preprocessors like SASS and different frameworks like Bootstrap and Foundation.

WHAT IS CSS?

Cascading Style Sheets (CSS) is a style sheet language for describing the display style of an HTML document. CSS is one of the most important web development technologies, especially for frontend development. The World Wide Web Consortium (W3C) developed CSS. It was first released almost 25 years ago in December 1996. The latest version of CSS is CSS3. The .css file extension is used for CSS files.

CSS was specifically designed so that content of a web page and the styling of a web page could be kept separate. Separating the content and the

DOI: 10.1201/9781003309062-3

presentation of a web page improves accessibility. It also helps in providing more flexibility and control over the presentation aspects of the web page. The presentation of a web page includes the layout, fonts, colors, etc. Adding all the styles in a single style sheet allows us to use the same style sheet for designing multiple pages. This reduces the complexity and also helps in removing repetition from the structural content. The CSS file can be cached, which will increase the page's loading speed when switching between pages that share the same formatting and styling.

WHAT IS NEW IN CSS3?

CSS3 is the latest addition to Cascading Style Sheets. CSS3 is the successor of CSS2 and aims to extend the functionalities of the previous version. There are many new features added to CSS3 like shadows, gradients, transitions, animations, rounded corners, etc. New layouts are also added, like multi-columns, flexbox, and grid layouts.

CSS3 Selectors

Selectors are the most basic yet necessary part of CSS. A CSS selector is used to select the HTML element you want to style. In previous versions of CSS, matching or selecting elements could only be done by type, class, or ID. CSS2.1 added different selectors by using pseudo-elements, pseudo-classes, and combinators. However, by using CSS3 you can easily target any element on the page. A wide range of selectors have been added in CSS3.

Attribute selectors were first introduced in CSS2. These selectors allow for matching elements based on the given attributes. The functionality and usage terms for these attribute selectors were further expanded in CSS3. Now, in CSS3 substring selection is also allowed.

1. Any element E with attribute attr and attribute value as val. The value of value should match with the beginning of the attribute value. Example – E[attr^=val]

2. Any element E with attribute attr and the attribute value ends in val. The value of the attribute value should match with the end of the attribute value. Example – E[attr$=val]

3. Any element E with attribute attr and the attribute value is valid anywhere. The value of the attribute value should match with the attribute value anywhere within the attribute. Basically, the attr should either be equal to val or a part of it at least. Example – E[attr*=val]

Pseudo-Classes

If you're already familiar with some of the pseudo-classes such as :link, :visited, :hover, :active, and :focus.

A few more pseudo-class selectors were added in version CSS3. The main class is the :root selector, which points to the root element of a document. In HTML, it could be <html>. Since :root is the main element, it allows a user to select the root element of an XML document without knowing its name. It also permits scrollbars when needed in a document.

As a complement element to the :first-child selector, the :last-child was added in CSS3. It can be used to select the last named element of a parent element. This rule would modify the font for the last paragraph of each article included in <div class='article'>/div> tags. Each article has a concluding paragraph with some information that needs to be universally stylized.

The :target pseudo-class selector was added as a new user interaction pseudo-class selector. When a user clicks on a same-page link, a rule like the first line below will function nicely; the link would look like the second line, and the highlighted span would look like the third.

A functional notation for selecting particular elements that fail a test has been created. The negation pseudo-class selector is almost any other selector that has been implemented. For example, if you want to put a border around images that do not have a border specified, use a rule like this.

CSS3 Colors

CSS3 supports different ways of describing colors. Prior to CSS3, we declared colors using the hexadecimal format (#FFF, or #FFFFFF for white). It was possible to declare colors using the RGB() (red, green, blue) notation, providing integers ranged from (0–255) or percentages.

The color keyword list has also been extended in the CSS3 color module to include 147 additional keyword colors (that are well supported). CSS3 also provides us with a number of options such as HSL, HSLA, and RGBA. The notable change with these color types is the ability to declare semi-transparent colors.

RGBA

RGBA works like RGB, it adds a fourth value: alpha, the opacity level or transparency level. The first three values represent red, green, and blue. For the alpha, 1 means fully opaque and 0 means fully transparent, and 0.5 is 50% opaque. You can use any number range between 0 and 1 inclusively.

HSL and HSLA

HSL is known as hue, saturation, and lightness. Unlike RGB, where you have to manipulate the brightness or saturation of a color by changing all three color values in concert, with HSL you can tweak either the saturation or the lightness while keeping the same base hue. The syntax for it is an integer value for hue and percentage values for saturation and lightness.

The hsl( ) declaration accepts three values:

The hue in degrees ranges from 0 to 359. Some examples are: 0 means red, 60 means yellow, 120 means green, 180 means cyan, 240 means blue, and 300 means magenta.

The saturation as 100% is the norm. This means 100% will be the full hue, and saturation of 0 will essentially give you a shade of gray.

A percentage for lightness with 50 being normal. A lightness of 100% means white, 50% will be the actual hue, and 0% will be black.

The a in hsla( ) also functions the same way as in rgba( ).

Opacity

In addition to specifying transparency with HSLA and RGBA colors (eight-digit hexadecimal values), CSS3 provides us with the opacity property. It sets the opaqueness of the element on which it's declared, similar to alpha.

Though the usage of both alpha and opacity notations seems similar, there is a main key difference in their function when you look at it.

A semitransparent RGBA or HSLA color has no effect on the element's other CSS properties or descendants, whereas opacity sets the opacity value for an element and all of its children.

Rounded Corners: Border-Radius

The border-radius property lets us create rounded corners without the images or additional markup. If you want to add round corners to your box, we simply add border-radius: 25px.

The border-radius property is a shorthand. For "a" element, the corners are all the same size and symmetrical. We can declare up to four unique values if we want different-sized corners.

Drop Shadows

CSS3 has the ability to add drop shadows to elements using the box-shadow property. The color, width, blur, height, and offset of one or more inner and/or outer drop shadows on your elements can be specified using this attribute.

Text Shadow

Text shadow provides shadows to individual characters in text nodes with text shadow. Prior to CSS3, this was accomplished by either utilizing an image or duplicating and positioning a text element.

Linear Gradients

It added the syntax for generating linear gradients with CSS3.

Radial Gradients

Gradients that are round or elliptical. Colors mix out in all directions from a starting point rather than advancing along a straight axis.

Images for the Background

CSS3 eliminates the need for a separate element for each background image, allowing us to use multiple background images on any element, including pseudo-elements.

CSS PREPROCESSORS

A CSS preprocessor is a tool that allows you to create CSS using the preprocessor's own syntax.

Although there are various CSS preprocessors to pick from, most will provide functionality that isn't available in pure CSS, such as mixins, nesting selectors, inheritance selectors, and so on. These characteristics make the CSS structure more readable and maintainable.

To utilize a CSS preprocessor, you must first install a CSS compiler on your web server. Alternatively, you can build the CSS preprocessor on your development environment, then upload the resulting CSS file to the web server.

Some of the popular CSS Preprocessors are listed below:

1. Sass

2. Less

3. Stylus

4. PostCSS

Preprocessors in CSS.

Sass

Sass (known for *syntactically awesome style sheets*) is a preprocessor scripting language that is interpreted or compiled into Cascading Style Sheets (CSS). It is the scripting language itself.

It consists of two syntaxes. Its original syntax, called "the indented syntax," uses the same syntax as Haml. It uses indentation to separate code blocks and newline characters to separate rules. The syntax "SCSS" (Sassy CSS) uses block formatting like that of CSS. It uses braces to denote code blocks and semicolons to separate rules within a block. The indented syntax and SCSS files are given the extensions .sass and .scss, respectively.

It consists of a series of selectors and pseudo-selectors that group rules that apply to them. Sass (in the larger context of both syntaxes) extends CSS by providing several mechanisms available in more traditional programming languages, particularly object-oriented languages, but that are not available to CSS3 itself. When SassScript is interpreted, it creates blocks of CSS rules for various selectors as defined by the Sass file. The Sass interpreter translates SassScript into CSS. Alternatively, Sass can monitor the .sass or .scss file and translate it to an output .css file whenever the .sass or .scss file is saved.

The indented syntax is a metalanguage. SCSS is a nested metalanguage, as valid CSS is valid SCSS with the same semantics.

SassScript provides the following mechanisms: variables, nesting, mixins, and selector inheritance.

Less

Less (Leaner Style Sheets stylized as Less) is a dynamic preprocessor style sheet language that can be compiled into Cascading Style Sheets (CSS) and run on the client-side or server-side. Alexis Sellier designed it, and it is influenced by Sass and has influenced the newer "SCSS" syntax of Sass, which adapted the CSS-like block formatting syntax. Less is an open-source project. Its first version was written in Ruby; in newer versions Ruby isn't used and has been replaced by JavaScript.

The syntax of Less is a nested metalanguage, as valid CSS is valid Less code with the semantics. Less provides mechanisms such as variables, nesting, mixins, operators, and functions; the main difference between Less and other CSS precompilers is that Less allows real-time compilation via less.js by the browser.

Stylus

It is a dynamic style sheet preprocessor language that is compiled into Cascading Style Sheets (CSS). It is influenced by Sass and Less. It is the fourth most used CSS preprocessor syntax. It was created by TJ Holowaychuk, a former programmer for Node.js and the creator of the Luna language. It is written in JADE and Node.js.

PostCSS

It is a software development tool that uses JavaScript-based plugins to automate routine CSS operations. It was designed by Andrey Sitnik with its origin in his frontend work for Evil Martians.

It is a framework to develop CSS tools. It can also be used to develop a template language such as Sass and Less.

The PostCSS core consists of:

- CSS parser generates an abstract syntax tree.

- It has a set of classes that comprises the tree.

- CSS generator which generates a CSS line for the object tree.

- Code map generator for the changes made in CSS.

Features are made available through plugins. Plugins are tiny programs that work with an object tree. After the core that has transformed a CSS string into an object tree, the plugins analyze and change the tree. Then the PostCSS generates a new string for the tree that was changed by the CSS plugin.

PostCSS and its plugins are written in JavaScript and distributed through npm and offer APIs for low-level JavaScript operations.

There are some official tools that make it possible to use PostCSS with build systems such as Webpack, Gulp, and Grunt. There is also a console interface available. The browserify or Webpack can also be used to open PostCSS in a browser.

CSS FRAMEWORKS

A CSS framework helps us in creating user friendly and mobile responsive web pages without any added hassle. A framework can be any software that provides a generic functionality and further add-ons. It contains features that allow the users to modify and customize according to their own needs. A CSS framework usually contains HTML and CSS at its core, so understanding those two becomes essential. It has self-explanatory components that anyone can quickly learn and implement. Most CSS frameworks essentially focus on mobile-first development. Mobile-first development means that while creating any web page, the primary focus is on how it is rendered on mobile devices. From there on, the user interface is scaled according to more giant screens. This approach is helpful as most users across the globe access internet using their mobile phones. Putting their needs first and ensuring that a website is working smoothly on any mobile device would increase traffic on any website.

Let's have a look at some of the most popular CSS frameworks.

Bootstrap

Bootstrap is one of the most popular frontend frameworks in the world. It is free and open source.

Advantages of Bootstrap

1. **Easy to use:** anyone with even a basic knowledge of HTML and CSS can create a full-fledged website using Bootstrap. It's that easy.

2. **Lightweight and customizable:** as a framework, CSS is incredibly light and can be customized according to one's needs.

3. **Mobile-first approach:** putting mobile devices first leads to an increased reach among the user base.

4. **Browser compatibility:** a consistent framework that supports all major browsers and their latest versions.

5. **Plugins:** there are several available JavaScript plugins to increase functionality that can be added according to one's requirement.

Disadvantages of Bootstrap

1. **Lack of uniqueness:** most Bootstrap websites tend to look the same, and even if you wish to change the inherent style, you need to rewrite many files and override the available styles, which can be time-consuming.

2. **Limited design options:** you need to put in extra effort and time to create a design unique to you.

3. **Verbosity:** styles created in Bootstrap tend to be verbose and generate a lot of output in HTML, which is usually deemed unnecessary.

Foundation

Foundation is an accessible framework that works for any device or medium. It has all the components required to create a web application like a responsive grid, buttons, typography, etc. It also has lots of impressive user interface (UI) elements. Foundation could be called a highly responsive and detailed network of frontend frameworks. You can easily plan responsive websites and applications using Foundation that would look great on any gadget. Foundation is also incredibly adaptable and adjustable as well as semantic and coherent. The user can start by designing a simple layout for small devices and can increase the complexity layer by layer as the application is scaled higher and higher. Foundation also provides support for RTL (right to left) languages. It is also Ruby on Rails friendly. It can be easily customized according to the needs and requirements of the users. It is used by some of the biggest names in the tech world like Adobe, Amazon, HP, etc. There is also a Foundation for Emails framework which is used to code responsive HTML emails.

Features

- Foundation offers a streamlined workflow which allows the developers to go straight from prototype to production. It makes it easy to write clean and semantic code from the very beginning.

- Foundation is built on Sass style sheet language, so it is easy to quickly customize the default style rules. There is also a simplified Sass setup process that requires fewer dependencies.

- The page load time is less.

- There is a selective import feature that saves a considerable amount of memory. It allows developers to choose only the components that they want to use.

- The Sass has an improved structure so as to avoid the unnecessary overcomplication of the CSS output. This leads to a leaner and cleaner codebase.

Tailwind CSS

Tailwind is a CSS framework that is used to make websites quickly and easily. It was first released in November 2017. Tailwind CSS is a utility-first CSS framework that is used for rapidly building custom user interfaces. It is a low-level CSS framework that is also highly customizable. It provides the user with all the building blocks they need to create a bespoke design. There are also no existing styles that you need to override in order to personalize and create your website according to your own choices. Tailwind does not impose strict design specifications on the users and hands them free rein so they can create the kind of site they want. For using Tailwind, the user simply needs to bring all these little components together so they can create a site of their liking with a unique interface. Tailwind just takes a raw CSS file and then processes that file over a configuration file and then produces an output.

Tailwind is a framework that highly prioritizes utility first with classes like text-focus, flex, pt-4, etc. Using these classes, you can create a website layout straight in your markup. It is increasingly adjustable because it works around utility classes. Working around utility classes also means that we can build custom designs without writing CSS the traditional way. Tailwind also has a faster UI-building process. Using Tailwind ensures that there are minimum lines of code in the CSS file. It also gives us the ability to customize the design and make our own components. It also makes the website responsive and helps us in making the changes in a desired manner. CSS is global in nature, so if you make a single change in a CSS file, it will get implemented in all the places the HTML file is linked with it. However, by using Tailwind CSS you can create local changes by using utility classes.

Features

- Tailwind CSS provides increased control over styling compared to Bootstrap. As Tailwind does not have a default theme like other CSS frameworks, it becomes easier to style web applications and websites. For example, you can choose to give a different look to each project even if you are using the exact same elements throughout. It is one of the few CSS-based frameworks that doesn't control how a user styles their websites and projects.

- When it comes to styling in HTML, there isn't a framework that is faster than Tailwind. You can create amazing-looking websites and layouts by styling the elements directly. Tailwind offers thousands of built-in classes which means you don't need to create designs from scratch. You don't need to write any CSS rules by yourself, and that is why creating and styling with Tailwind is so fast.

- Tailwind is responsive and also provides additional security. Tailwind is a mobile friendly CSS framework which allows you to design the layout directly in an HTML file.

- Even though Tailwind CSS is fairly new, it has proven to be a stable framework since its initial release.

- Tailwind has the ability to create lightweight, responsive themes for web applications. It uses Purge CSS to remove all the unused CSS classes from the final version. This helps in making the final CSS file as small as possible.

CHAPTER SUMMARY

In this chapter, we learned about CSS3 and its various properties. We talked about what's new in CSS and the various preprocessors. We also discussed some popular CSS frameworks. In the next chapter, we will talk about JS and jQuery.

JavaScript and jQuery

IN THIS CHAPTER

- ➤ JavaScript/ ECMAScript Fundamentals

- ➤ Using Third-Party Libraries

- ➤ jQuery Libraries and Patterns

- ➤ JAM Stack Generators

In the previous chapter, we talked about CSS3. We learned about CSS and what is new in CSS3. We also talked about all the different selectors available in CSS and what is the purpose of each one of them. We also learned about different preprocessors like SASS and how they work. We also discussed different CSS frameworks like Bootstrap and Foundation. In this chapter, we will discuss JavaScript, one of the core technologies behind frontend development. We will also talk about ECMAScript and its fundamental concepts. We will learn how to use third-party libraries and discuss the various jQuery libraries and patterns. In the end, we will learn about JAM Stack generators like VuePress and Hugo.

WHAT IS JAVASCRIPT?

JavaScript is a text-based, interpreted programming or scripting language that enables us to add advanced functionality to any web page. JavaScript is incredibly lightweight and is mostly used for scripting web pages. It is also used to build web applications that interact with the client without reloading the page every time.

DOI: 10.1201/9781003309062-4

89

The majority of dynamic websites you encounter on the internet employ at least some JavaScript. JavaScript is used whenever a website displays timely content updates, interactive maps, 2D or 3D graphics, a scrolling movie, or even a simple button that does something when you click on it. The DOM API is used to change the user interface with JavaScript. It accomplishes this by dynamically altering the HTML and CSS.

DOM stands for Document Object Model. The DOM is a cross-platform, language-independent interface that operates by constructing a tree structure from HTML content. Every node of the tree is an object that represents a section of the document in this case. A document is represented as a logical tree in the document object model. Each branch of the tree has a node at the end, and each node has an item.

DOM gives us programmatic access to a tree, which we may utilize to change the structure of the tree further. Changing the structure of the tree always entails changing the document's inherent behavior. The Document Object Model (DOM) is used to manipulate a page and change its behavior. Not only can the DOM be used to change the document's structure, but it can also be used to change the document's style and content. Attaching event handlers to nodes allows you to control the DOM. An event handler is called whenever an event is triggered.

The impact that JavaScript has on the web is unmatched. It is estimated that more than 97% of the websites available on the internet use some form of JavaScript on the client-side for displaying any type of web page behavior. In fact, JavaScript is considered one of the essential stepping stones towards learning web development. The prerequisite for learning JavaScript is a basic understanding of HTML and CSS. JavaScript's popularity stems from the fact that it is versatile and flexible enough to be utilized on both the client and server sides.

JavaScript was mainly designed for creating network-centric applications. It is open as well as a cross-platform programming language. It is a language that is complementary to Java and can also be integrated with it. At the same time, it is also complementary to HTML and can also be integrated with it.

In real-world applications, DOM produces a document, such as an HTML page, by constructing a tree-like structure within the web browser. Every document's nodes are arranged in a tree structure. A DOM tree is the name for the tree structure. The "document object" is the node at the very top of the tree.

Any browser that renders an HTML page downloads the HTML code into its local memory and then parses it automatically to show the page on the screen. The browser constructs a DOM of the page after it is loaded. The document object model that was constructed would represent the HTML document in an object-oriented manner. It would then serve as a conduit between JavaScript and the document.

A dynamic web page is built in this manner. Any element or its characteristics can be modified, added to, or removed using JavaScript. It can modify any element's CSS style. It can also generate new events while reacting to all existing ones at the same time.

Although a DOM tree is commonly used to display HTML documents, it is not required. Some browsers do not display documents as trees and instead use internal models. Each browser has its own set of models.

JavaScript logo.

How Does JavaScript Work?

JavaScript language is a scripting language that can work both on the client-side and server-side. There are additional tools and languages that help JavaScript when it comes to working on the server-side. So, in this section, we will only discuss how JavaScript works on the client-side as JavaScript is primarily used for that. JavaScript is incredibly efficient and is one of the most commonly used scripting languages. The word client-side scripting language refers to any language that works on the client-side. The term client-side could also be referred to as client machine.

The scripting language works inside the web browsers. However, for a scripting language to work in a web browser, it is very important for the web browser to support JavaScript or be JavaScript enabled. Most web browsers these days support JavaScript or have their own JavaScript engine. Like Google Chrome has its own JavaScript engine called V8. Node.js is also built on the V8 engine of Google Chrome. Microsoft Edge has a JavaScript engine named Chakra, Safari has JavaScript Core and the JavaScript engine of Firefox is called Spidermonkey. JavaScript can be used in many ways; it just depends on the web developers how they want to use it and for what purpose. One of the most common ways JavaScript is used is for validating data given by the user in the form fields.

Whenever we run a JavaScript code in our web browser, the JavaScript engine pertaining to that web browser understands the code and then eventually runs it. JavaScript also happens to be an interpreted language which means that each line of the code gets executed one by one instead of compiling the whole program all at once. So, the JavaScript engine will take each line of the code, convert it, and then run it in the same order.

Whenever a JavaScript program runs inside the web browser, the JavaScript code is received by the browser engine and then the engine runs that code to obtain the output. In any standard JavaScript engine, the source code needs to go through several steps in order to get executed. A JavaScript engine has different parts that help us in executing the code. Now, let us look at those different parts and understand what function each one of them performs

1. **Parser:** whenever we run a piece of JavaScript code, our code first gets to the parser inside the JS engine. The parser checks the code for syntactic errors, going through each line because it is an interpreted language. So, whenever an error is detected, the execution stops right there, and an error is thrown.

2. **AST:** it stands for Abstract Syntax Tree. After the parser checks the code and there are no mistakes in it, a data structure is created called AST.

3. **Machine Code Conversion:** once the syntax tree is created by the parser, the JS engine converts the JavaScript code into machine code. Machine code is the language that the machine can understand.

4. **Machine Code:** at last when the program is finally converted into machine code, it gets sent to the system for execution, and then that machine code is run by our system.

JavaScript
Client-side
Client JavaScript on the client-side is the most common type of language. The text must be embedded or referenced in an HTML document in order for the code to be translated by the browser.

It means that a web page should not be a standalone HTML, but can include user-friendly programs, browser controls, and dynamic HTML content.

In comparison to typical CGI server scripts, the JavaScript client-side technique has numerous advantages. You can use JavaScript to verify that a user has provided a legitimate email address in a form field, for example.

When the user submits the form, JavaScript code is employed, and only valid entries are transferred to the web server.

User-initiated events, including button clicks, link navigation, and other explicit and implicit user activities, can be activated with JavaScript.

Advantages

- JavaScript always gets executed on the client-side regardless of where you host it. It saves lots of bandwidth and makes the execution process faster.

- XMLHttpRequest is an important object in JavaScript that was designed by Microsoft. The object call that is made by XMLHttpRequest is an asynchronous HTTP request made to the server. It helps in transferring data to both sides without reloading a page.

- One of the major perks of JavaScript is that it has the ability to support all modern browsers. It also produces an equivalent result in every browser.

- JavaScript also receives support from the biggest companies in the world by creating projects. Like Google created Angular framework, in the same way Facebook (now Meta) created the React.js framework.

- It is ubiquitous as it is used everywhere on the web.

- It works great with another language as well thus, it can be utilized in various types of applications.

- There are lots of open-source projects available that help the developer.

- Lots of community support and courses are available online to learn JavaScript easily and quickly.

- It allows creating rich interfaces.

- It is versatile, so you can create a whole JavaScript app from front end to back end using just JavaScript

Disadvantages

- It may be difficult to develop large applications solely on the basis of JavaScript. You might have to use the TypeScript overlay.

- It is applied to mostly large frontend projects. The configuration is tedious as the number of tools that are required to create an environment for such a project is a lot. That is why it is sometimes directly associated with the library's operation.

- The main disadvantage of JavaScript is that the code can be viewed by anyone.

- No matter how fast JavaScript interprets, the DOM is comparatively slow and can never render fast enough with HTML.

- If some error occurs in JavaScript, then it can even stop the whole website. And this happens even though the browsers are extremely tolerant of errors in JavaScript.

- It is usually interpreted differently by different browsers. This makes it somewhat complex to read and write the browser code.

- Even though some HTML editors do provide the debugging feature, it is still not as efficient as other editors for languages like C and C++. It makes it difficult for the other developer to detect the issue.

- The conversions take a longer time when converting a number to an integer. This not only increases the time needed to run the script but also reduces the overall speed.

JavaScript, once again, is a lightweight interpreted computer language that lets you add interaction to otherwise static HTML websites.

ECMAScript 6

ECMAScript 2015 or ES2015 is a special update to the JavaScript language. It is the first major update to the language since ES5 which was developed completely in 2009. Therefore, ES2015 is often called ES6.

We will look at different things available in ES6.

1. ES6 Syntax

In ES5, when declaring a variable using the keyword var, the width of the global or local variable. When you declare a variable without function, the range of the variable is global. The range of local variables depends on their scope.

ES6 offers a new way of declaring dynamics using the key let. The keyword let is similar to the keyword var, except that these variables are restricted width.

Example – let variable_name

Varieties of var

- In the creative phase, the JavaScript engine assigns storage spaces to variable variables and immediately launches them to define them.

- In the performance phase, the JavaScript engine assigns varies to var the values specified by the shares if available. Otherwise, the vari variable of var remains undefined.

Let variables

- In the creative phase, the JavaScript engine assigns dynamic storage spaces but does not launch the dynamics. Non-implemented flexible navigation will create a ReferenceError.

- The let variable has the same action phase as var var.

The temporary dead spot starts from the block until the declaring declaration is processed. In other words, it is an area or place where you will not be able to access the dynamics before they are defined.

ES6 provides a new way of consistent advertising using the keyword const. The const keyword creates a read-only reference for the value.

Legally, fixed identifiers are capital letters. Like the keyword let, the const key announces a variable width restriction. However, the block-scoped variables declared by the const key cannot be reshared.

The variables declared the key let let change. It means you can change their prices whenever you want.

However, the variables created by the const keyword are "unchangeable." In other words, you cannot reset them to different values.

If you try to redistribute a different pronounced cons key name, you will get TypeError. Unlike the keyword let, you need to initiate a number of variables declared by the const key. The const key ensures that the variable you create is read-only. However, it does not mean that the actual value at which the variable reference of the const cannot be changed.

2. **Destructuring**

- Array destructuring
- Object destructuring

3. **ES6 Modules**

In JavaScript, the term "modules" refers to small units of private code, reusable. They are the basis of many JavaScript design patterns and are essential for building any JavaScript-based application.

In simple terms, modules help you write code in your module and specify only those parts of the code that should be accessible to other parts of your code.

JavaScript has long modules. However, they were used in libraries, not built on language. ES6 is the first time JavaScript has built-in modules.

- Each JavaScript module is a piece of code that is used when a JavaScript file has been uploaded.

- In that code, there may be announcements (variables, tasks, classes, etc.).

- By default, all declarations in that file remain in place in that module and cannot be accessed in other modules unless the module file exports them.

What Are ES6 Modules?
Prior to this module, it was not possible to directly reference or insert one JavaScript file into another, so developers turned to other options such as multiple HTML tags. This is a bad practice as each script launches a new

HTTP application, which affects page performance and interrupts further processing while it is running.

Suppose we have a file, app.js, and included in this file is a function that checks every limit on a number and returns it if it is EVEN or ODD. This function is now only available in app.js. Wherever you need this function, you must rewrite the work or paste the text again. This is where the ES6 Modules come in.

Prior to the release of ES2015, there were at least three major levels of competition:

1. Asynchronous Module Definition (AMD)

2. Requires JS modules

3. CommonJS Modules

Therefore, the standard single, native module was proposed in ES6 (ES2015). ES6 modules are a very powerful concept. Although support is not available everywhere at the moment, the most common way to use them is to accumulate in the ES5. You can use Grunt, Gulp, Webpack, Babel, or another transpiler to integrate modules during the construction process. Transpilers, or source-links, are tools that read source code written in the same programming language and generate the same code in another language.

4. **ES6 Classes**

Classes are a model for creativity. They combine data with code to work on that data. Classes in JS are built on prototypes but also have specific syntax and non-shared semantics and ES5 semantics similar to the class.

Defining Classes
Classes are actually "special tasks," and just as you can define performance talks and job announcements, the class syntax has two parts: class talks and class announcements.

Class Announcements
Another way to define a class is to use a class announcement. To announce a class, you use a class keyword with a class name.

Classroom discourse is another way to describe a class. Classroom presentations can or may not be named. The name given to the class expression refers to the place in the body of the class. However, it can be achieved with the place of the name.

The body of the class is part of the folded brackets {}. This is where you describe class members, such as methods or builders.

Strict Mode

The body of the class is made up of solid mode that is, the code written here is under strict syntax for additional functionality, some quiet errors will be cast, and some keywords are reserved for future versions of ECMAScript.

Builder

The builder method is a special way of creating and implementing a class-created object. There can be only one path with the word "builder" in the classroom. SyntaxError will be dropped if the class contains more than one developer method event.

The builder can use a large keyword to call a superclass builder. Vertical keyword describes a vertical path or class structure. Strong members (structures and methods) are called without confirmation of their class and cannot be named, for example, class. Standby methods are often used to create application functions, while static features are useful for cache, configuration, and any other data that you do not need to duplicate in all cases.

5. **Arrow Functions**

The functions of the arrow have a few important differences in the way it works that separate it from normal functions, as well as a few practical enhancements. The biggest difference in performance is that the arrow functions do not have this binding or prototype and cannot be used as a builder. Arrow functions can also be listed as a more integrated alternative to normal functions, as they provide the ability to leave brackets in the parameters and add a short working body sense with a vague return.

There is a big difference between the function of the arrow and the normal function.

6. First of all, in the arrow function, these, arguments, super, new.targ et are lexical. It means that the arrow function uses these variables (or constructions) from the closed lexical width.

7. Second, the arrow function cannot be used as a function construc-tor. If you use a new keyword to create something new in an arrow function, you will get an error.

8. **Symbols**

A symbol is a built-in object that the constructor returns with an old sym-bol – also called a symbol value or just symbol – that is guaranteed to be different. Symbols are often used to add unique structural keys to an object that will not conflict with the key or any other code that can add to an object and hidden in any of the other ways other code often uses to access an object.

Every Symbol () call is surely to return a unique Symbol. Every Symbol .for call ("key") will always return the same Symbol with a given "key" value. If Symbol.for ("key") is called, if the Symbol with the given key can be found in the global symbol register, that token is restored. If not, a new Symbol is created, added to the Global Symbol registration under the given key, and then restored.

9. **Iterators and Generators**

In JavaScript, an iterator is something that defines a sequence and maybe a return value when disconnected.

Specifically, an iterator is any object that uses an Iterator protocol by having the following method () which returns an object with two characteristics:

number

The next value in the multiplication series.

done

This is especially true if the last digit in the track has already been used. If the value is close to the transaction, the repetition value is multiplied.

Once created, a recurring object can be clearly repeated by the next repeated call (). Repeating over the iterator is said to consume the iterator because it is usually possible to do it only once. After the discount value has been deducted, the extra calls to the next () must proceed with the {done: true} return.

The most common JavaScript iterator is the Array iterator, which returns each value to the same associated members in sequence.

Although it is easy to assume that all repetitions can be expressed as frames, this is not true. The arrays should be provided in full, but the iterators are only used if necessary. Because of this, duplicates can produce unlimited size sequences, such as the value range between 0 and infinity.

10. **Promises**

A promise is a representation of an unknown value when a promise is made. It allows you to associate holders with the success rate of a consistent action or reason for failure. This allows non-compliant methods to return values as synchronized methods: instead of returning the final amount immediately, the inconsistent method returns the *promise* of providing value at some future point.

The promise is in one of these provinces:

- **pending:** initial status, unfulfilled or rejected.

- **fulfilled:** which means the work was successfully completed.

- **rejected:** which means that the operation failed.

A pending promise can be *fulfilled* in value or *rejected* for a reason (error). When any of these options occur, the corresponding holders listed in the promised manner are called. If the promise has been rejected or fulfilled when the holder is attached, the holder will be called, so there is no racing mode between the completion of the corresponding operation and its handles attached.

11. **ES6 Collections**

ES6 introduces four new data structures that will add power and brightness to the language: Map, Set, WeakSet, and WeakMap.

Map is the first building/data collection we will explore. Keyboard maps and values of any kind. It is easy to create new maps, add/remove values, attach keys/values and accurately determine their size.

Sets are a set of price lists that may not contain duplicates. Instead of being identified as frames, sets are accessed using keys. Sets are already available in Java, Ruby, Python, and many other languages. One difference between ES6 Sets and those in other languages is that order is important for ES6 (not so in many other languages).

The JavaScript Garbage Collection is a type of memory management where objects that are no longer addressed are automatically removed, and their resources recovered.

Map and Set pointers in objects are strictly controlled and will not allow garbage collection. This can be costly if the maps/sets refer to large items that are no longer needed, such as DOM items already released from DOM.

To address this, ES6 also introduced two new weaker clusters called WeakMap and WeakSet. These ES6JavaScript collections are "weak" because they allow unwanted items to be removed from the head. WeakMaps is similar to regular maps, although there are a few exceptions and differences mentioned above regarding garbage collection. WeakMaps has a few popular usage features. They can be used to store confidential data, and can be used to track DOM nodes/items.

WeakSets Set Collections whose elements can be collected in the trash when references are no longer needed. WeakSets does not allow duplication. Its use cases are limited (for now, at least). Many first responders claim that WeakSets can be used to mark items without modifying them. ES6-Features.org has various examples of adding and removing elements to WeakSet to track whether things are marked or not.

12. **Array Extensions**

13. **Object Extensions**

14. **String Extensions**

15. **Proxy and Reflection**

THIRD-PARTY JAVASCRIPT

Third-Party company JavaScript is a JavaScript program that allows for the creation of highly distributed web applications. Unlike standard web applications, which are accessed at a single web address (http://yourapp .com), these applications can be downloaded incorrectly from any web page using simple JavaScript integration.

You may have encountered JavaScript on a third party before. For example, consider ad texts, which produce and display targeted ads on publishers' websites. Ad text may not be popular with users, but it does help web publishers to earn a living and stay in business. They are visible on millions of websites, yet almost all of them are third-party content offered on various ad servers.

Ads scripts are just one use; developers look to third-party scripts to solve a number of issues. Some use them to make independent products that meet the needs of the publishers. For example, Disqus, a web-based startup in San Francisco — and an employer of the best authors of this book — is developing a third-party comment app that gives web publishers a quick comment system. Others develop third-party documentation to expand their standard web applications to reach audiences on other websites. For example, Facebook and Twitter have created dozens of social media widgets that are uploaded to publishers' websites. These widgets help social networks to engage their users outside of their normal ecosystem applications. Others develop third-party documentation to expand their standard web applications to reach audiences on other websites. For example, Facebook and Twitter have created dozens of social media widgets that are uploaded to publishers' websites. These widgets help social networks to engage their users outside of their normal ecosystem applications.

Small companies can also benefit from JavaScript third-party JavaScript. Suppose you are the owner of a B2B (business-to-business) web application that handles web forms to collect information from your customers. You have a chance that customers who would like to use your app are reluctant to redirect their users to an external website. With JavaScript third-party software, you can get customers to upload your form request directly to their web pages, solving their redirecting concerns.

External company JavaScript is not everything. Writing these apps remotely is no small feat. There are a lot of traps and scams you will need to overcome before you can send JavaScript to a third party that will capture its own in the wild. Fortunately, this book will show you how to guide you through the full development of a complete third-party application.

But before we dive into JavaScript third-party content, you need to learn the basics. This chapter will better define JavaScript for third-party software, look at real-world land use from a few companies, move on to the easy-to-use third-party application, and discuss the many challenges facing third-party development.

In standard software exchanges, there are two groups. There is a buyer, or first person, who uses the software. The second part is the provider or author of that software.

You might think of a company as the first user to use a web browser on the web. The browser requests a content provider when they visit a website. That provider, the second company, transfers HTML webpage, images, style sheets, and text from their servers to the user's web browser.

A simple web exchange like this can only be two groups. But many website providers today include content from other sources or third parties. External companies may offer anything from the content of the article (Associated Press), to image processing (Gravatar), to embedded videos (YouTube). In a strict sense, anything offered to a client provided by a non-website provider is considered an external company.

When you try to use this definition in JavaScript, things get muddy. Many developers have differing opinions about what constitutes JavaScript third-party content. Some define it as any JavaScript code that isn't written by the supplier. This will include popular libraries such as jQuery and Backbone.js. It will also enter any code that you have copied and pasted from the website for software solutions such as stack overload. Any and all unencrypted code will be subject to this definition.

Some refer to JavaScript third-party content as code provided from third-party servers, not under the content provider's control. The argument is that the code hosted by content providers is under their control: content providers choose when and where the code is used, have the power to modify it, and are responsible for maintaining its conduct. These differ from the code provided by the various third-party servers, your content may not be changed by the provider, and may change without notice.

Third-Party JavaScript

Usage

We detected that the third-party JavaScript is a code used on someone else's website. This gives the third-party code access to the HTML objects of that website and the JavaScript content. You can then manipulate that page in many ways, including creating new DOM features (Document Object Model), installing custom style sheets, and registering browser events to capture user actions. For the most part, third-party documents may do any work that you can use JavaScript on your website or application, but only on someone else's behalf.

Equipped with the power of remote web page fraud, the question remains: what is it worth? In this section, we will look at some of the conditions for using the real world of third-party documentation:

- **Embedded Widgets:** Small interactive applications embedded in the publisher's web page

- **Statistics and Metrics:** Collection of information about visitors and how they interact with the publisher's website

- **API Wrappers Web Services:** By developing client applications that connect to external web services

Embedded widgets (usually third-party widgets) are probably the most common way to use third-party documentation. These applications are usually small, interactive, made accessible to the publisher's website, but they upload and send resources to or from a different set of servers. Widgets can vary greatly in complexity; they can be as simple as a picture of the weather in your area, or they can be as complex as an instant messaging client with full features.

Widgets allow website publishers to embed apps on their web pages with minimal effort. They are usually easy to install; more often than not, publishers only need to insert small HTML captions into the source code of a web page to get started. Completely based on JavaScript, widgets do not require the publisher to install and maintain any software that works on their servers, which means minor maintenance.

Some businesses are fully committed to the development and distribution of embedded widgets. Earlier, we talked about Disqus, a San Francisco-based web launcher. Disqus develops a comment widget that works as part of commenting for blogs, online publishing, and other websites. Their product is run almost entirely by a third-party JavaScript. It uses JavaScript to download comment data to the server, to comment as HTML on the page, and to scan form data for other commenters — in other words, everything. It is embedded in websites using HTML captions that include five lines of code.

Disqus is an example of a product that is only used in its distributed form; you will need to visit the publisher page to use it. But widgets are not always independent products like this. Generally, they are "portable" extensions for common, common home-based web applications.

For example, consider Google Maps, which is undoubtedly the most popular maps app on the web. Users browse at https://maps.google.com to view interactive maps of places around the world. Google Maps also provides traffic and public transportation, satellite imagery, and even street view using local photography.

Surprisingly, all this magic also comes with widget flavors. Publishers can embed a map program on their web pages using captions of the JavaScript code found on the Google Maps website. On top of this, Google provides a set of public works for publishers to edit map content.

CHAPTER SUMMARY

This chapter taught us about JavaScript and jQuery and how it works and learned about their uses. In the next chapter, we will talk about JavaScript and Frontend Development.

Frontend Development and JavaScript

IN THIS CHAPTER

➢ Uses of JavaScript in frontend development

➢ jQuery Plugins in frontend development

➢ Working with React and Angular

In the previous chapter, we talked about JavaScript and jQuery. We discussed the fundamentals of both JavaScript and ECMAScript and learned about third-party libraries and JAM Stack generators. In this chapter, we will talk about frontend development and JavaScript.

JavaScript and frontend development go hand in hand. There are three main components required when it comes to developing the front end of any website: HTML, CSS, and JavaScript. Each of these latest technologies plays a crucial role in making a webpage what it is. We have already discussed the role of HTML and CSS in detail in the previous chapters. The focus of this chapter, therefore, would be JavaScript.

USES OF JAVASCRIPT IN FRONTEND DEVELOPMENT

A frontend developer's role is to create code and markup to be rendered by the web browser. Anything that a client sees while visiting a webpage is controlled by the developer. Gone are the days when websites only displayed static content. JavaScript has totally changed the game.

DOI: 10.1201/9781003309062-5

Interactivity

HTML provides the structure, CSS brings out the looks, and JavaScript is what powers the interactivity. It's only one of the numerous things JavaScript can accomplish. The general interactivity of any site is created and maintained because of it. All of it can be done using JavaScript, from building rich UI components like image sliders, tabs, accordions, and pop-ups to creating subtle bits and pieces here and there for an immersive experience.

It also provides additional functionality to any site that is not easily achievable by HTML and CSS. Let's say you click on a checkbox in a form. Depending on the checkbox you selected, a pop-up is displayed asking you another question based on your previous answer. Unlike JavaScript, displaying choice-based output cannot be achieved because it allows web pages to respond to user activity and dynamically update themselves. All of this is done without even reloading the page.

AJAX

AJAX stands for Asynchronous JavaScript and XML. It allows web pages to interact with a web server in the background. With the help of AJAX, parts of a web page can be updated without reloading the whole page. You can request as well as receive data from the server after the page has been loaded. It is not a programming language. It simply uses a combination of a built-in XMLHttpRequest object in the browser to request data from the web server. And to display the data, it uses JavaScript and HTML DOM.

Whenever an event occurs on a web page, XMLHttpRequest is created with the help of JavaScript. The event that triggers the response could be loading a new page, clicking a button, pressing a specific keyboard short-cut key, etc. The XMLHttpRequest object then proceeds to send a request to the web server, and the server processes the request upon receiving it. The web page receives a response from the server. The response is read by JavaScript, and proper action is taken according to the received response. This is how AJAX creates a seamless experience between the user and the web application.

Creating Web Applications

JavaScript is used for making robust web applications. There are lots of JavaScript frameworks available these days, like Angular, React, and Vue.j s, that make it very easy to build complex SPAs. SPA stands for single-page web applications. Developers can easily use these JavaScript frameworks to create mobile apps. A JavaScript framework is basically a collection of JavaScript code libraries that supply pre-written codes to the developer. This pre-written available within the framework will help them in creating features and tasks in routine programming. There are lots of popular apps that are made using JavaScript, like Netflix, Uber, LinkedIn, etc. There are lots of companies that use Node.js, which is a JavaScript-based runtime environment. It is built on Google Chrome's JavaScript V8 engine.

Creating Mobile Apps

Mobile devices are everywhere these days, and they are the ones that are used for accessing the internet by a vast majority of the population. These days most of the internet users use their mobile devices to surf the web. JavaScript is so versatile that we can create apps with it that are not even web based in the first place. We can easily build an application for non-web contexts using JavaScript. JavaScript has such varied features that it can be used as a powerful tool for creating web applications. One of the most popular JavaScript-based frameworks for mobile app development is React Native. React Native allows you to create natively rendered mobile apps for Android and iOS.By using React Native, you can create an application for various platforms by using the same codebase for all of them. We do not need to write different codes for Android and iOS. React Native follows "WORA," which stands for Write Once, Run Anywhere. WORA is used to describe the ability of a program to be just written once and then run on any platform. This term was first coined by Sun Microsystems in reference to Java.

Building Web Servers

A web server can easily be created using Node.js. Node.js is an open-source, cross-platform, backend-based runtime environment in JavaScript. It runs on Google Chrome's JavaScript V8 engine and helps us in executing JavaScript code outside of a web browser. With Node.js, you can write command-line tools. And when you are doing server-side scripting, you can run your script on the server-side and produce dynamic web page content. All of this could be accomplished without even sending the page to the user's browser. Using Node.js also helps in maintaining the "JavaScript everywhere" paradigm for developers. This paradigm is based on the notion that all of the web applications' fundamental components are unified and written in a single language rather than several languages for server and client scripts separately.

Node.js has an event-driven architecture that is also capable of asynchronous I/O. Asynchronous I/O refers to a form of input/output processing in which processing of other stuff continues before the transmission has finished. Asynchronous I/O is also called non-sequential I/O. The need for asynchronous I/O arises because input and output operations (I/O) on any computer can be incredibly slow when compared to the processing of data. This is a simple approach to I/O that leaves the processor idle. Asynchronous I/O, also called a blocking I/O, starts an operation first and then waits for it to complete fully so as to move on to the next task. But using this method blocks the progress of any program while the communication is still in progress as the system resources sit idle. When any program makes lots of I/O operations, it means that, for the most part, the processor is just sitting idle, waiting for the input/output processes to complete. This is why asynchronous input/output is the preferred method of input/output processing because it is faster and saves up a lot of time and resources.

As mentioned before, Node.js is an event-driven architecture which means it does not wait for the response sent by the previous call. It just moves on and starts processing the next call. The servers that are created using Node.js are fast and transfer chunks of data in one go without constantly buffering. If you wish to create a server in Node.js, you can use the HTTP module to do so and create a server by using the createServer() method. The HTTP module contains the function that is used to create a web server. This method gets executed whenever someone tries to access the port 8080. As a response to this, the HTTP server displays HTML. Also, it should be included in the HTTP header. As we already know, a web server accepts requests from clients such as web browsers. In order to interact with a web server, we need to enter a domain name, which would then get translated to an IP address (IP stands for Internet Protocol) by a DNS server (DNS stands for Domain Name System). An IP address is actually a unique set of numbers that is used to identify a machine on the internet. Just like your fingerprint, each device accessing the internet has a unique IP address.

Web Development

JavaScript is one of the most important steps for anyone that wants to become a web developer. JavaScript is most popularly used for making interactive web pages. It helps us in adding dynamic behavior to a web page. It also helps us in adding any kind of special effects to any type of web page. On most websites, JavaScript helps with validation purposes.

JavaScript helps us in executing some complex actions that make the clients easily interact with the websites. By using JavaScript, a website can possibly load content into a document without even loading the web page.

Presentations

JavaScript is also capable of creating presentations as a website. There are various such libraries available that can help us create a web-based slide deck like RevealJS, BespokeJS, etc. They are relatively easy to use, so you can easily create something incredible in a very short span of time. RevealJS is mostly used to create interactive and beautiful slide decks. It works with some help from HTML. These presentations work not only well on desktops but also on mobile devices and tablets as well. It also supports all kinds of CSS color formats. On the other hand, BespokeJS includes a wide variety of features like bullet lists, responsive scaling, etc.

Cross-Browser Compatibility

There are a variety of browsers in the industry, and they run on a variety of operating systems and devices. Each of these browsers has its quirks and bugs as well. Even though all browsers follow the W3C compliance standards, still certain issues do come up here and there. Let's take, for example, a website that applies a certain CSS styling rule that works well in all browsers except one. So, in this case, what the developers do is, instead of rewriting the whole section, they target that one browser. They try to find a solution for that specific browser. This is done by using JavaScript libraries such as Modernizr, which helps in isolating code specific to a browser. The developers can leverage the scripts, write new styling rules that work, and resolve the issue.

Plugins

Plugins are used as add-ons in a website or web application to enhance its capabilities. There are lots of JavaScript plugins available, and they can be easily dropped into a site. A plugin does not require much modification to function properly. You just need to configure certain options to set it up. A third-party JavaScript plugin is used for adding features like banner ads, chat support, social sharing, etc.

Frameworks and Libraries

A framework is a tool that provides readymade components to speed up the development time. There are dozens of JavaScript frameworks available in the market that can be used for various purposes. Building a web app or a website from scratch is a tedious task in itself. Using a framework eases the burden to some extent. Some of the popular JavaScript frameworks are React, Angular, and Vue.js.

A library consists of pre-written JavaScript code that allows for the easier development of web applications. It contains various objects, methods, and functions to perform certain tasks on a web page. Using a library makes the whole development process smoother for a web developer as the code can be reused and repurposed. There are lots of libraries available, each used to perform a specific function. For example, Galleria is a popular JavaScript library that is used for making slideshows.

JQUERY PLUGINS IN FRONTEND DEVELOPMENT

As we discussed above, a plugin is a software component that is added to a software program to provide functionality or support for certain features. It is added as an independent module that helps in customizing an application.

On the other hand, a jQuery plugin is a method that is used to extend jQuery's prototype object. It is a piece of code written in a JavaScript file and enables all jQuery objects to inherit methods that you add. Before discussing jQuery plugins in detail, let's get to know jQuery first.

jQuery is a library of JavaScript that is used by web developers to add functionality to their websites. It mainly simplifies the interaction between the HTML elements and the JavaScript code. jQuery takes common tasks that would require writing many lines of JavaScript code and wraps them into methods. These methods can be called with a single line of code, thus reducing both development time and memory usage. It also simplifies complicated things from JavaScript like DOM manipulation and AJAX calls. jQuery runs on the "write less, do more" concept. This concept makes the code simple, concise, and reusable. Not just the traversal of the HTML DOM tree is simplified, but the handling of events, animation, and ajax support in web applications also gets easier.

jQuery uses a combination of web technologies like HTML, JavaScript, CSS, and AJAX. These are all markup-based technologies that work together perfectly. It uses a simple, clean, albeit powerful syntax, which makes it easy to select the DOM elements on a website page. It has loads of utility functions that help in array manipulation, trimming, coding string iteration, etc. These functions help in assimilating jQuery and JavaScript beautifully. One of the perks of jQuery is that it will render elements even if JavaScript is disabled for any reason. You can display animation and also be SEO friendly. As the pages get loaded faster with jQuery, the website ranking gets boosted further.

In order to add jQuery, all you need to do is add the reference file within the <head> section of the HTML document. You have the option of using a CDN (Content Delivery Network) or hosting the jQuery library yourself by placing the downloaded file in the same directory as the pages where you want to use it. You can reference that inside the <script> tag, which would be inside the <head> tag.

- **Code:**

```
<script type="text/javascript"
src="//ajax.googleapis.com/ajax/libs/ jquery/3.5.1/
        jquery.min.js">
</script>
```

OR

```
<script src="jquery-3.5.1.min.js"></script>
```

Creating a jQuery Plugin

Let's say that you want to create a single method that you can call on a jQuery selection; then, it would perform a series of operations on that selection. In order to create a personalized plugin, you need to create one of your own. There are certain files that provide useful jQuery methods that can be used alongside the jQuery library methods. To enable a plugin method, first include a plugin file at the head of your HTML document that is quite similar to the jQuery library file. Make sure that it appears after the main jQuery source file but also right before our custom JavaScript code. The positioning of the code matters as it would determine how the page would render. If our plugin file is named debug.js, we need to include it in our HTML like it is shown below.

- **Code:**

```
<script src = "jquery.debug.js" type = "text/
            javascript">
</script>
```

The jQuery method that we are creating acts as the plugin. You can define both the variables and the methods. Both of them can be either private or public inside the plugin. The syntax for creating a method within a plugin file the same is as follows:

- **Code:**

```
$.fn.methodName = function(){
//method definition
};
```

There are certain things to keep in mind while creating a method.

1. If you attach any method or function, each of them should have a semicolon at the end.

2. You should always add a plugin to jQuery's namespace with $. .fn

3. The method that you use must return the jQuery object, and if it does not, then at least it should be explicitly noted.

4. To iterate over the current set of matched elements, you should use "this. each()."

5. Use $.noop function instead of using empty functions inside plugins.

Let's try to change the text color to red and implement that using a plugin. For that, we need to write the following method in the file debug.js

- **Code:**

```
$.fn.makeitred = function() {
   this.css ("color", "red");
   return this; //not a required step, but recommended
};
```

In the HTML, add the plugin inside the <head> tag.

- **Code:**

```
<script src = "jquery.debug.js" type = "text/
                javascript">
```

```
</script>
<script type = "text/javascript" language =
              "javascript">
    $(document).ready(function() {
      $("p").makeitred();
    });
</script>
```

The above code will change the content inside the <p> tag of the HTML <body> into red color.

Features of a jQuery Plugin

1. You can implement chaining, which refers to calling another function or plugin on the same returned results, all within one line of code.

- **Code:**

```
$("p").makeitred().addClass( "active" );
```

2. In order to use the $ jQuery alias and also work well with other plugins, you need to put all of your code inside an Immediately Invoked Function Expression. Pass the function jQuery and name the parameter $ like

- **Code:**

```
(function ( $ ) {
   $.fn.makeitred = function() {
      this.css( "color", "red" );
      return this;
   };
}( jQuery ));
```

You can also declare private variables and hide the custom color. This leads to encapsulation.

3. When writing plugins, take up one slot within $.fn and use parameters to control the action a slot performs. This reduces the plugin footprint.

- **Code:**

```
(function ( $ ) {
    $.fn.changecolor = function ( action ) {
        if ( action === "active") {
        this.css ( "color", "red" );
        }
        if ( action === "inactive" ) {
        this.css ( "color", "blue" );
        }
 return this;
    };
} ( jQuery ));
```

4. A jQuery object usually contains references to any number of DOM elements, and that is why they are also referred to as collections.

- **Code:**

```
(function ( $ ) {
    $.fn.makeitred = function () {
        this.filter( "a" ) .each (function () {
            this.css ( "color", "red" );
        });
        return this;
    };
} ( jQuery ));
```

5. For creating empty functions use $. noop functions

- **Code:**

```
options = $.extend ({
 // ...,
 onItemClick: function () {},
 onItemOpen: function () {},
 onItemClose: function () {}
}, options);
Instead of these empty functions, you should define
                                    like this:
options = $.extend ({
```

```
// ...,
onItemClick: $.noop,
onItemOpen: $.noop,
onItemClose: $.noop
}, options);
```

6. You can pass plugins as a series of options to change the way they work. These options get passed to HTML as a series of key-value pairs

- **Code:**

```
$( "div" ).makeitred({
    color: "orange"
});
```

To give the plugin the ability to process options, use the extend method.

- **Code:**

```
(function ( $ ) {
    $.fn.makeitred = function( options ) {
        // This is the easiest way to have default
                options.
        var settings = $.extend({
            // These are the defaults.
            color: "#ff0000",
            backgroundColor: "white"
        }, options );
        // Make the collection colour based on the
                settings variable.
        return this.css({
            color: settings.color,
            backgroundColor: settings.backgroundColor
        });
    };
}( jQuery ));
```

7. Event listeners can be seen as callback functions when they are called at a specific moment. The callbacks work when they are triggered. Here is an example of mouseover() and mouseout() events

- **Code:**

```
(function($){
  $.fn.extend({
    animateMenu: function(options) {
      var defaults = {
animatePadding: 60,
      defaultPadding: 10,
 };
 var options = $.extend(defaults, options);
    return this.each(function() {
  var o = options;
  var obj = $(this);
  var items = $("li", obj);
  items.mouseover(function() {
   $(this).animate({paddingLeft: o.animatePadding},
         300);  }).mouseout(function() {
   $(this).animate({paddingLeft: o.defaultPadding},
         300);
  });
    });
    }
  });
})(jQuery);
```

The following code will help the animateMenu() plugin to work:

```
<head>
<script type="text/javascript">
$(document).ready(function() {
$('#menu').animateMenu({animatePadding: 30,
defaultPadding:10});
});
</script>
</head>
<body>
<ul id="menu">
<li>Home</li>
<li>Posts</li>
<li>About</li>
<li>Contact</li>
</ul>
</body>
```

Need for a jQuery Plugin

jQuery is one of the most popular JS libraries out there. It works on all the latest browsers and is easy to learn and use. It requires much less code compared to other libraries. Using the basic syntax script, a user can choose from a wide variety of animation effects. Most mobile devices also support animations created using jQuery over those made with Flash. It is a newly developed program and has better adaptability for various mobile versions.

To keep the codebase lean and light, most of the functions have either been omitted or moved to the plugin section. If you want to add the omitted features, then you can use them as plugins. Because of the lean library, the coding is kept at a restricted level and helps in saving the bandwidth for faster loading. Also, there is no dearth of jQuery plugins on the internet, so it is easy for developers to create special effects.

One of the biggest reasons behind choosing jQuery plugins over JavaScript implementations is the fact that it prevents function conflicts by automating the extension of functions within the plugins. It also provides reusability, encapsulation, and chaining. Plugins can also be used for SEO which makes the website user friendly. It also makes it faster and easier to navigate. If a developer has a strong grasp of jQuery plugins, they can make development much easier and quicker.

React

React (also known as React.js or ReactJS) is a free JavaScript package that allows you to construct UI-based interactivity. Meta (previously Facebook) and a community of individuals and businesses are hosting the event. With a framework similar to Next, React may be used as a foundation for developing single-page, mobile, or server-based apps. However, React is only concerned with the management of the country and providing that status to the DOM, so creating React applications often requires the use of additional libraries to route, as well as some client-side functionality.

Basic Use

The following is a bizarre example of using React in HTML with JSX and JavaScript.

```
import React from "react";
Const Greeting = () => {
 return (
```

```
  <div className = "hello_world">
   <h1> Hello, Earth! </h1>
  </div>
 );
};
```

Automatically export Greetings:

The greeting work is part of the React showcasing the famous introduction to "Hello, world"

When viewed in a web browser, the following will appear:

```
<div class = "hello_world">
 <h1> Hello, Earth! </h1>
</div>
```

Components

The react code is made up of organizations called components. These components can be reused and must be created in the SRC folder according to the Pascal Case as its name change (capitalize camelCase). Parts can be delivered to a specific section in the DOM using the React DOM library. When donating a portion, one can transfer values between components using "props":

```
import React from "react";
import Tool from "./ Tool";
const Example = () => {
 return (
   <>
    <div className = "app">
     <Tool name = "Gulshan" />
    </div>
   </i>
 );
};
```

Automatically export example:

In the example above, the prop name with the value "Gulshan" was transferred from the Example section to the Tool section.

Two main ways to advertise segments in React are through working-class and class-based components.

Class-based components

Class-based segments are announced using ES6 classes.

```
Parent CategoryPrevious section React.Component {
 shape = {color: 'green'};
 give () {
  return (
   <ChildComponent color = {this.state.color} />
  );
 }
}
```

When class sections are concerned with the use of classrooms and life cycle approaches, functional sections have a hook to deal with the state administration and other issues that arise when coding React.

Visible DOM

Another notable feature is the use of a virtual Document Object Model or virtual DOM. React creates a database of memory data, calculates the resulting difference, and updates the displayed DOM of the browser properly. This process is called reconciliation. This allows the editor to write code as if the entire page is assigned to each change, while the React libraries only provide subsections that actually change. This optional offer offers great performance enhancement. Saves effort to recreate CSS style, and page layout.

Lifecycle Methods

Class-based lifecycle methods use a hooking method that allows coding at fixed points during half-life.

- ShouldComponentUpdate allows the developer to prevent unnecessary partial retrieval by false retrieval if the provision is not required.

- componentDidMount is called when the component is "mounted" (the component is already created on the user interface, usually by combining it with the DOM node). This is often used to activate data uploads from a remote source via the API.

- partWillUnmount is called immediately before the portion is demolished or "reduced." This is usually used to relieve the need for a service is a component that cannot be removed by partial reduction (e.g., to remove any setInterval ()-related component cases, or "eventListener" edited "document" due to component presence).

- render is the most important part of the life cycle and is the only one needed in any part. It is usually called when the status of the component is updated, which should appear in the user interface.

React Hook

Hooks are functions that allow engineers to "connect" to the response and life cycle features from the operating components. Hooks do not work within classes – allowing you to use React outside of classes.

React offers a few built-in disciplines such as use State, Context, Reducer, Memo, and UseEffect. More is written in the Hooks API Reference. State and UseEffect are the most widely used, state-of-the-art control and adverse effects respectively.

Some Rules

There are hook rules that define the code pattern of the feature on which hooks rely. It is a modern way of handling the situation with React.

- Hooks should only be called at a high level (not internal locks or if statements).

- Hooks should only be called on React working parts and custom hooks, not regular operations or class components.

- Although these rules will not apply during operation, code analysis tools such as linters can be modified to detect multiple errors during development. The rules apply to both the use of hooks and the use of custom hooks, which can cost some hooks.

ReactJS or simply React is the most used frontend-based JS framework. It is also free and open source and is used for building dynamic user interfaces based on UI components. It was developed and currently maintained by Meta, formerly known as Facebook. It is capable of creating and handling web pages with high incoming traffic. React is mostly used for state management and rendering that state to DOM. It uses virtual DOM and integrates the same with any other application. React does the manipulation with the virtual DOM in the memory before it makes any final changes within the DOM of the browser. It is done so that it only changes what needs to be changed. React was first released for public use in July 2013 and was created by Jordan Walke.

Characteristics

- React is used to create dynamic and interactive UI for mobile and web applications. It is also capable of rendering the right components efficiently in case there is a change in network speed.

- It has declarative views that make the code readable and incredibly easy to debug.

- For every DOM object, React creates a virtual DOM object. A virtual DOM object is created by making a virtual copy of the original DOM and is used as a representation of the primary DOM.

- React has a W3C object model event system that is also fully compatible.

- React also provides a cross-browser interface to any native event. It means you don't need to worry about incompatible event names and fields.

- JSX is a markup syntax that makes writing React components easier. It makes the syntax almost identical to the HTML injected into the web page.

- React uses an application architecture called flux controls. React updates the View for the user, and Flux controls the application workflow. Virtual DOM will compare the new data with the original data and update the View automatically.

- React Native is used as a custom renderer for React, and it makes use of the native components instead of the web components.

- Everything is seen as the component of the web page in React. A View or the UI is created by combining all the components together. A component is used to define the visuals in ReactJS.

Angular

It is a frontend-based web application framework written in TypeScript. It is free and open source, and it is operated by Google. Angular is also part of the MEAN stack. Apart from Angular, the MEAN stack uses MongoDB database, Express.js as a web application server framework, and Node.js as a server runtime environment. Angular is mostly used for developing a single-page application, also called an SPA. Angular extends the HTML into the application and interprets the attributes in such a way as to perform data binding.

Why Do We Need Angular?

Angular is a client-side JavaScript framework that may be used to create bespoke HTML, CSS, and TypeScript apps. Misko Hevery and Adam Abrons founded AngularJS in 2009 as a Google project. Because of its MVC (Model-View-Controller) feature, it is a frontend JavaScript framework that makes it simple to create adaptable web-based applications. Although AngularJS is still maintained as a framework, it is no longer developed or updated.

With sophisticated applications that are difficult to maintain in JavaScript and JQuery. We need a way to process our application. That is why these frameworks (Angular, React etc.) are used.

The fact that Angular employs TypeScript as its programming language is one of its most notable characteristics. Angular applications can also be written in languages like Dart or JavaScript. However, TypeScript remains the major programming language.

Why Use Angular

- Angular is a popular framework for building web and mobile applications and can be an excellent framework for building large, powerful, and easy-to-use web applications. So here's a list of reasons why you should use Angular:

- Security. Angular is a trusted forum because it is supported by Google.

- Reduced development time. Angular relies on the current JavaScript machine for converting templates into code. Angular loading time and fast.

- The unit is ready for testing. Angular combines two methods for combining module data and components, making the code consistent and easy to understand in unit testing. Every unit of code is independently tested throughout the application process, providing deep quality control.

- Cross-platform. Angular-based PWAs can work on a variety of platforms, and the framework is widely used in native mobile applications. Previously, frontend developers used the Angular cross-platform combo platform. Today, its most popular combination is NativeScript.

- Complex learning curve. Angular uses a more complex learning curve than other frameworks. To get started, you need to test all the features of the framework, such as RxJS (a functional compatible development library) and TypeScript (used to maximize storage and code support), not just JavaScript.

- The community. Angular has a large community and an ecosystem that is continuously supported. There is plenty of content in the framework such as guidelines and videos, as well as many useful tools for third parties.

Features

- Capable of delivering an app-like experience through a web platform while also maintaining a high standard of performance.

- No installation is required for such web apps and can also provide the functionality to work offline.

- Usage of strategies from Cordova, Ionic, or NativeScript to build a native app.

- Using the same methods to create a web app, desktop-installed apps can also be created for Mac, Windows, and Linux.

- Angular can turn templates into code that is highly optimized and gives the benefits of handwritten code.

- Capable of serving the first view of .NET, PHP, Node.js, and other similar servers for almost instant rendering in HTML and CSS.

- Angular apps load quickly and deliver automatic code-splitting so users can load the code they require to render the view they request.

- Angular can easily create UI views with a simple yet powerful template syntax.

- Angular command-line tools help in building apps quickly, adding required components fast, and instantly deploy them.

- Angular is popular enough, so most IDEs and editors provide intelligent code completion and instant error feedback.

- Protractor helps in making scenario tests run faster and in a stable manner.

- Angular's intuitive API helps in creating high-performance animation timelines with very little code.

- Angular helps in creating accessible applications that have ARIA-enabled components and developer guides for the same.

CHAPTER SUMMARY

In this chapter, we learned about the uses of JavaScript in frontend development and saw all the different ways JavaScript can be put into use. From creating servers, games to various frameworks, all of it can be done using the language. We dove deeper into a JavaScript library named jQuery. It is a very popular library, and we learned what it is used for and also created a plugin with it. In the end, we discussed a bit about how React and Angular work and their features. In the next chapter, we will take a look at Code Optimization. Why it is important, what are its goals and the advantages as well as disadvantages of it.

Code Optimization

IN THIS CHAPTER

- ➤ What is Code Optimization
- ➤ Goals of Code Optimization
- ➤ Category of Optimization
- ➤ Code Optimization Techniques

In the previous chapter, we learned about JavaScript and its use within Bootstrap components. We talked about several Bootstrap components like attributes, alerts, transitions, carousels, etc. We also discussed jQuery plugins available in Bootstrap and how previous versions of Bootstrap used jQuery as a dependency. We also learned how to integrate Bootstrap with React and Angular. In this chapter, we will talk about code optimization. We would learn about the best practices for writing code, how to write cleaner and lighter code and how to best optimize it.

WHAT IS CODE OPTIMIZATION?

In this era where technology is changing rapidly, there has been a demand for lightweight, low power consuming, and responsive applications. Some examples of such applications include graphic editors on mobile devices, video calling/conferencing applications, live broadcasting stations, and many other devices just like that. This type of need is directly related to the fact that apps should make optimal use of CPU resources such as audio processing, video processing, compute engine, crypto engine, and so on,

DOI: 10.1201/9781003309062-6

in order to achieve the optimal result. However, this type of demand raises a unique challenge for developers, which forces them to write the program in a well-structured manner. This is done to utilize each CPU clock cycle to its full potential. The application program or the embedded software primarily runs on processors with minimal computational power. This limited power hence raises the evident need for code optimization.

Most of the compilers today optimize the program code at the lowest level. However, manual optimization remains essential for optimizing at the source code level. The compiler is often limited to general-purpose optimization so that it applies to many programs at once. This forces the programmer to get creative and use their knowledge and experience so that optimization is performed. It is often challenging to identify the areas where more optimization is most required. This is even more so in the case of extensive and complex applications. In cases like that, we need to use the profiler to identify those areas that require optimization. After placing, the result of the optimization is verified. There are lots of different techniques by which a program can run faster, but it often increases the program's size.

Software applications, at their core, are designed to achieve a specified set of functionalities that the developers want. The performance consideration is also added to the design later in the development process. Several techniques can help any software run faster. But to achieve speed improvement, there is also a downside; an increase in the size of the application. So, to solve this issue, the developers need to write the program code in such a way that optimizes both the memory and the speed. There are other ways to obtain performance statistics, but the ideal one is to utilize a competent performance profiler, which displays and analyzes the time spent in each function.

Code optimization refers to the process of improving the code in such a way that it consumes fewer resources and works faster than before. Modifying software or some part of it to make it work quicker and more efficiently is the primary goal of code optimization. Optimizing a computer program could consume less memory storage space or CPU, draw less power, etc. Code optimization is also referred to as program optimization and software optimization.

Any method of code modification could be termed code optimization if it ends up improving the quality and the efficiency of the code. There are multiple reasons why any program or computer software needs to be optimized; it could decrease its size to consume less memory. Optimization helps reduce the number of input and output operations so that the code executes more quickly.

All optimization methods should comply with one essential requirement, and that is, the output for both optimized and non-optimized programs must be the same. This requirement can be ignored in exceptional cases where changes in the inherent behavior of the optimized code lead to better features. The consequences of changing the behavior of a program while optimizing it can be ignored if the changes end up creating a better result.

Different types and levels of optimization are used depending upon a case in point. Optimization can be performed manually by a programmer or by an automatic optimizer. An automated optimizer could be specialized software, or it could be a built-in compiler. Most modern processors can also optimize the code based on their execution order or code instructions.

The optimizations are further classified into two types: high-level and low-level optimizations. Low-level optimizations are performed later on when the source code has already been compiled into a set of machine instructions. At this level, automated optimization comes into play. On the other hand, all the high-level optimizations are done by a programmer. A programmer is usually entrusted with that.

GOALS OF CODE OPTIMIZATION

1. Remove repetitive code without changing the meaning of the program

2. Reduce execution speed

3. Reduce the consumption of memory

There are several points that you need to keep in mind before attempting to optimize the program code:

Time-based optimization will result in faster output, but it can also increase the size of the codebase. So, if you try to optimize the code for time-based performance, it may start conflicting with the memory and size consumption of the program. To avoid such a scenario, you need to find a delicate balance between the time taken and memory consumed while also keeping your requirement in mind. Trying to optimize the performance is a never-ending process. There are always different ways to improve your code and run it faster. Sometimes, we may feel tempted to use specific programming methods over others to make our code run faster at the expense of not following the best coding practices. Try to avoid any such kind of methods as much as possible. It will make it harder to maintain the code in the long run.

CATEGORIES OF OPTIMIZATION

1. Space optimization

2. Time optimization

Because both space and time optimization categories are interrelated, you can optimize your code by lowering either space or time. Space optimization is usually performed manually, which is an incredibly time-consuming process and may lead to results that are not optimal depending upon the programmer and their skills. For time-based optimization, always take some time to think about the proper algorithm to use. Always try to avoid type conversion and use the same variables as much as possible. Instead of making a loop run faster, make sure to make the loop run as little as possible. If a loop runs for lots of cycles in your code and takes up most of your execution time, then redesign the code.

CODE OPTIMIZATION TECHNIQUES

Some of the most critical code optimization techniques are:

1. **Compile Time Evaluation:** two methods fall under this category.

    i. Constant Folding: This technique involves folding the constants. The expressions with constant value operands are evaluated at compile time. Those expressions are then replaced with their results.

    ii. Constant Propagation: If a constant value is assigned to a variable, then the variable would get replaced with the constant value during compilation.

2. **Common Sub-Expression Elimination:** it is the expression that has been computed before but somehow appears again during computation. In this technique, the common expressions are removed. The common expressions are removed so as to avoid re-computing them

all over again. The result that has already been computed is used in the program further.

3. **Code Movement:** this technique involves the movement of the code. The code within the loop is moved outside. This is done so that the code does not get executed again each time the loop runs. Removal of this code saves time and resources.

4. **Dead Code Elimination:** in this technique, the dead code is eliminated. The code statements whose outputs are never used are eliminated in this method.

5. **Strength Reduction:** in this technique, the strength of the expressions is reduced. In this technique, the expensive operators are replaced with cheap ones.

CHAPTER SUMMARY

In this chapter, we learned about code optimization and the goals behind optimizing a piece of code. We also learned about the different categories of code optimization. And in the end, we learned about the various techniques used for optimizing code. In the next chapter, we will learn how to integrate Bootstrap with Jekyll and ASP.NET; we also learned how APIs work in Bootstrap.

Appraisal

W<small>EB DEVELOPMENT HAS TWO</small> main parts: frontend and backend. Frontend development is also called client-side web development. In this book, we discussed frontend development in detail. It mainly entails creating web pages or web applications for the client using HTML, CSS, and JavaScript. Anything that appears on the client-side is something that the users can interact with.

Frontend development is a constantly evolving field. The tools and techniques keep on changing. The developer needs to always be ready to learn a new skill as the market is very volatile. With every new library or framework that is coming out, the developer needs to constantly upskill themself. Awareness about how the market is developing is also important.

The objective of any developer behind designing a website is to make sure that whenever a user opens up a site, the information is arranged in such a format that the relevant information is easy to find. However, it becomes more difficult for the developer because there are now so many devices with different screen sizes and resolutions. The developer has to take these aspects into consideration so as to design a website suitable for every user. A website should render correctly for every browser (cross-browser), various operating systems (cross-platform), and different devices (cross-device).

In order to be a frontend developer, a person has to learn how to architect and develop websites and applications using web technologies. These applications operate on the Open Web Platform. They can also act as compilation input for non-web-based platform environments like React Native. Anyone who enters the field of web development has to learn HTML, CSS, and JavaScript. These three technologies are deemed as the core. These three can be used in different runtime scenarios, which are explained below.

1. **Web Browsers:** It is a piece of software that is used to retrieve, traverse, and present information on the world wide web. Browsers usually run-on desktop, laptop, computer, mobile phone, tablet, etc. The most used web browsers across the globe are Chrome, Safari, Internet Explorer, Firefox, and Edge.

2. **Headless Browsers:** Headless browser is a type of web browser that does not have a graphical user interface. These browsers are controlled from the command line interface programmatically. Mostly these types of browsers are used for web page automation, functional testing, scraping, unit testing, etc. You can retrieve and traverse web pages straight from the command line. Commonly used headless browsers are Headless Chromium, Zombie, and slimerjs.

3. **Webviews:** It is used by a native operating system in a native application to run web pages. Webview is like a single tab from a web browser that is embedded within a native application running on any device like iOS, Windows, Android, etc. For webview development, there are some applications that are most commonly used. Cordova is mainly used for native phone and tablet apps. For desktop apps, typically, NW.js and Electron are used.

4. **Native:** nowadays, a frontend developer can use the knowledge that they have gained through creating web pages for browsers to craft code for an environment that is not mainly fueled by a browser engine. Certain environments like Flutter and React Native use web technologies without web engines to create native applications.

Let's look at some popular terms that are used in frontend development

- **Web Page:** A web page is a hypertext document that can be displayed in any web browser like Chrome, Firefox, Safari, Edge, etc. A web page is also commonly referred to as a page.

- **Website:** A website is simply a collection of web pages. All of these web pages are interconnected and grouped in a way that the user can move from one page to another. It is often referred to as a site.

- **Web Server:** A web server is a computer that is used to host websites on the Internet. It is essentially a computer software with suitable hardware that is used for accepting requests via HTTP. A user initiates communication by making a request, and the server responds to it.

- **Web Browser:** A web browser, simply referred to as a browser, is application software that is used for accessing any type of content available on the world wide web. The web server obtains the required content from the web server whenever a user requests a specific web page or website, and the browser subsequently shows that page on the user's screen.

- **Search Engine:** A search engine and a web browser are often confused with each other, but they are different things. A search engine is mainly a website that helps you find other web pages by providing links to other websites. However, in order to access web pages through a search engine, you need a web browser.

- **Internet:** The Internet is a global system of computers connected to each other that use TCP/IP, also called the Internet Protocol Suite, to communicate with each other. The Internet is a collection of interconnected networks. It offers a wide range of information and services, such as email and file sharing.

  The Internet can be considered as the infrastructure, and the web is a service that is built on top of that infrastructure. The Internet began as a research project of the United States Army in the 1960s. This research project then further evolved as many public universities and private companies joined the network. The public infrastructure of the Internet that we access today came into being in the 1980s. Simply put, the Internet is a way to make all the computers connected to each other no matter what happens.

  In order for two computers to connect with each other, we need to link them. This link could be physically or wirelessly. Physical links are usually done with an Ethernet cable, whereas wireless links happen through Bluetooth or Wi-Fi. All modern computers are capable of sustaining both of these types of connections.

- **Intranet:** Intranet refers to private networks that can only be accessed by members of a particular organization. They are used for sharing resources, collaborating, and communicating among members of that organization.

  Extranet: Extranets are similar to Intranet, the only major difference being they are open to all or part of a private network that helps in collaborating with other organizations as well. They are mostly used to share information safely and securely with members of that group like clients or stakeholders. The function of Extranet is almost the same as Intranet, like sharing files, collaborating, discussion boards, etc.

- **TCP/IP:** TCP stands for Transmission Control Protocol, and IP stands for Internet Protocol. These are nothing but a suite of communication-based protocols that are used to connect devices on the Internet. TCP/IP are also used as communication protocols in both Intranet and Extranet. TCP and IP are two main protocols in the suite, but there are other protocols included in it as well. The TCP/IP protocol suite acts as an abstraction layer between the Internet applications and the routing and switching fabric.

  TCP/IP is used to specify how the data would be exchanged over the Internet for end-to-end communications. The protocol identifies how data should be broken into packets, transmitted, routed, and received at the destination. It needs very little central management, and it is designed to make networks reliable so that they can recover quickly and automatically if a device on the network fails for some reason.

- **Packet:** Packets are the basic unit of communication used in a TCP/IP network. The devices available on the TCP/IP network divide the data into smaller pieces for easier transmission. Breaking down data into small pieces allows the network to accommodate various bandwidths. This helps in creating multiple routes to a single destination. In case certain pieces of data get lost or interrupted on their way to their destination, then those packets can be retransmitted. Each piece of data is considered a packet. A packet is a term that can be used interchangeably with a datagram. A packet can be seen as a smaller fragment or segment of a larger message.

- **Client-Server Model:** The client-server model is a distributed application structure that works by partitioning tasks or workload between servers and clients. Servers are seen as the providers of a resource or service, whereas clients are seen as the service requesters. In the client-server architecture, when the client computer sends a request for data to the server through the Internet, the server accepts it. The request is processed, and the data packets are delivered back to the client. Clients do not share any of their resources with the servers. Examples of the client-server model are email, World Wide Web, etc.

IP Address: An IP address is a one-of-a-kind identifier for every device connected to the Internet or a local network. "Internet Protocol" is what IP stands for. It is a set of rules and directives that govern the type of data that can be sent through the Internet or a local network.

Essentially, IP addresses are simply used as identifiers that allow information to be sent between various devices on a network. These IP addresses contain information pertaining to the location of the user and make devices accessible for communication. The Internet also needs a mechanism to distinguish between different sorts of devices, such as computers, routers, and webpages. IP addresses give a means of doing so, making them an important aspect of how the Internet functions.

An IP address is simply a series of digits separated by colons or periods. IP addresses are divided into two types: IPv4 and IPv6. IPv4 uses four sets of three numbers each to create a user's IP address. It uses periods to separate one set of numbers from the other. Each set can only have a number between 0 and 255. On the other hand, in IPv6, a 128-bit address method is used. A set of numbers are separated from each other using a colon.

- **DNS Server**: DNS resolution is the process of converting a hostname (for example, www.example.com) into a computer-friendly IP address (such as 191.178.18.71). Every device connected to the Internet is assigned an IP address. That address is required to locate the relevant Internet equipment, just as a street address is required to locate a specific residence. When a user types example.com into their web browser, a translation must take place between what the user types and the machine-friendly address required to reach the example.com webpage.

- **HTTP**: HTTP is also known as Hypertext Transfer Protocol. It is a protocol that offers a set of rules and standards that govern how any information can be transmitted through the Internet on the World Wide Web. HTTP mainly provides standard rules for web browsers and web servers to communicate.

HTTP is a network protocol for the application layer, and it is built on top of TCP. It uses Hypertext structured text to establish a logical link between two nodes that contain text. It is also referred to as a "stateless protocol" as each command is executed separately, without using the reference of the previous run command.

- **HTTPS:** HTTPS is also known as Hypertext Transfer Protocol Secure. It is a highly advanced protocol. It is also a more secure version of HTTP. HTTPS uses port no. 443 for data communication purposes. It allows secure transactions by encrypting the entire communication with SSL. To provide an encrypted and secure identification of a network server, HTTPS combines the SSL/TLS protocol with HTTP.

HTTP also allows the server and browser to establish a secure encrypted connection. In both directions, data security is provided. It assists you in preventing the abuse or theft of potentially sensitive information such as bank account information.

SSL transactions are negotiated using a key-based encryption method in the HTTPS protocol. The strength of this key is usually 40 or 128 bits.

Now, we will see how the three core technologies work together for frontend development.

HTML

HTML or Hypertext Markup Language is a standard markup language that is used to display documents in a web browser. It is mainly used to provide a structure to a web page so that content is aligned in a user-friendly way. This helps in viewing the document online in a browser.

As it is a markup language, it is made up of tags. Everything that is done in HTML is done with the help of tags. There are various tags that help in displaying text, ordered lists, unordered lists, tables, forms, etc. Any HTML document contains two main sections: head and body. Metadata which is used to describe the page is contained inside the head section. On the other hand, the body section includes all the tags that are used for representing visual content on any web page.

HTML is a full platform independent language. It can be used on any platform like Windows, Linux, Mac, etc. Web browsers receive the HTML pages from the web server or from local storage. The documents received are then rendered into multimedia web pages. In HTML, the elements are the building blocks of any web page. Images, hyperlinks, and interactive forms can also be embedded within a page.

There are multiple versions of HTML. The latest version is HTML 5. it has features like canvas, web socket, native audio, video support, geo-location, etc. HTML is an extremely simple language to use. Anyone can create an HTML file using a text editor and simply execute it in a browser.

Pros

- It is widely used.

- It is supported by every browser.

- It is easy to learn and use.

- It is incredibly lightweight and loads fast.

- It is free.

- No need to purchase any extra software.

- It runs on any browser or operating system.

- It has a loose syntax.

- Easy to write and code even for programming beginners.

- Allows for the utilization of templates which makes designing a web page easier.

- Useful for beginners who want to get into the web designing field.

- It is supported by each and every browser out there.

- HTML is built on every website.

- It is used for data storage like the XML syntax.

- It has various tags and attributes for different purposes, which shorten your time of coding.

Cons

- It is a static language, so it cannot produce any dynamic output.

- Creating the structure of an HTML document is difficult.

- Even a small error can sometimes disrupt the whole flow of the web page.

- Creating an HTML web page from scratch is time consuming.

- It takes time to create a color scheme for any web page and to make lists, tables, and forms out of it.

- As it is a static language, you can only create plain and static pages with it.

- Just to make a simple web page, you'll need to write a lot of codes.

- There are not many security features offered by HTML.

- As you need to write a lot of codes, even for basic stuff, it creates some complexity.

- You need to check for deprecated tags and not use them. Other languages like CSS and JavaScript have taken over the functionality of that tag.

CSS

CSS or Cascading Style Sheets is a style sheet language that is used for describing the style of presentation of an HTML document. CSS is considered as one of the core technologies for web development, primarily for frontend development. It provides control to the web designers about how a website communicates with the web browsers. It includes the formatting and display of the HTML documents.

It is a text-based coding language that is used to specify the website format. It defines the way a site could communicate with the web browser. By using CSS, web developers can regulate different style elements and functionalities.

CSS was developed by the World Wide Web Consortium (W3C). It was first released almost 25 years ago in December 1996. The latest version of CSS is CSS 3. The .css file extension is used for CSS files.

CSS was specifically designed so that content of a web page and the styling of a web page could be kept separate. Separating the content and the presentation of a web page improves accessibility. It also helps in providing more flexibility and control over the presentation aspects of the web page.

The presentation of a web page includes the layout, fonts, colors, etc. Adding all the styles in a single style sheet allows us to use the same style sheet for designing multiple pages. This reduces the complexity and also helps in removing repetition from the structural content. The CSS file can be cached, which will increase the loading speed of the page when switching between pages that share the same formatting and styling.

Pros

- Less complex, which reduces the collective effort required to style a web page considerably.

- Reduces the file transfer size.

- CSS provides the ability to re-position content. It helps in determining the changes within the position of web elements.

- By using CSS, a developer can easily specify a style for an element once and repeat it multiple times throughout the web page. It will automatically apply that required style.

- One style sheet can be reused across various websites and web pages.

- It simplifies the maintenance of code as you need to make the required changes only once in the style sheet, and it will reflect all across the website.

- It uses few lines of code, which increases the site speed.

- Less complex, so the effort is reduced.

- Helps in creating spontaneous and consistent changes.

- The changes made with CSS are device friendly.

- Helps in creating a responsive design with media queries so the websites can run smoothly on multiple devices.

- Easy to customize a web page.

- It helps in removing insignificant tags from the main page.

Cons

- The CSS that works with one browser might not work properly for another browser.

- There are different versions of CSS, which might create confusion.

- In terms of security, CSS is not the best.

- Browser compatibility for different versions is dubious at best.

- There are multiple levels which are bound to create some confusion among new developers.

- CSS works differently in certain browsers like IE and Opera support CSS as a different logic.

- There might be some cross-browser issues.

- After making changes, we also need to confirm the compatibility.

Here are some of the popular CSS frameworks.

BOOTSTRAP

Bootstrap is a free and open-source CSS-based framework. It is used to create mobile-first responsive websites. It is one of the most popular frontend frameworks in the world. As of August 2021, it is the tenth most starred project on GitHub. Bootstrap essentially contains components which you can use to create design templates. These components use CSS and sometimes JavaScript as well. For example, forms, buttons, navbar, etc.

Mark Otto and Jacob Thornton initially created Bootstrap. It was released for the first time more than ten years ago, in August 2011. Since then, many changes have been made, and improved versions have been released. The latest stable version was released in October 2021, and it is called Bootstrap 5. It was initially called Twitter Blueprint as both Mark and Jacob used to work at Twitter and wanted to create a framework that would help them maintain consistency across the platform. However, utilizing multiple different libraries to make the user interface resulted in inconsistencies and differences across the platform. It was also proving difficult to maintain the code. This duo of a developer and a designer then came up with Bootstrap.

Bootstrap has a very popular 12-column grid system that helps in quickly building layouts. The grid system is fully responsive and has six breakpoints on the basis of screen resolution. Bootstrap also has a huge number of pre-built components that the users can modify according to their needs by using the additional classes provided.

Bootstrap Features

- Create full-fledged responsive websites in a short time

- Create mobile-friendly websites

- Quick and automated optimization according to different websites

- Create dynamic web pages

- Manage a large amount of content

- Create tooltips and popovers to show hint text

- Create carousel and image slider

- Create different types of forms and alert boxes

Advantages of Bootstrap

- **Easy to use:** anyone with even a basic knowledge of HTML and CSS can create a full-fledged website using Bootstrap.

- **Lightweight and customizable:** as a framework, CSS is incredibly light and can be customized according to one's needs.

- **Mobile-first approach:** putting mobile devices first leads to an increased reach among the user base.

- **Browser compatibility:** a consistent framework that supports all major browsers and their latest versions.

- **Plugins:** There are several available JavaScript plugins to increase functionality that can be added according to one's requirement.

Disadvantages of Bootstrap

- **Lack of uniqueness:** most Bootstrap websites tend to look the same, and even if you wish to change the inherent style, you need to rewrite many files and override the available styles, which can be time consuming.

- **Limited design options:** you need to put in extra effort and time to create a design unique to you.

- **Verbosity:** styles created in Bootstrap tend to be verbose and generate a lot of output in HTML, which is usually deemed unnecessary.

TAILWIND CSS

Tailwind is a CSS framework that is used to make websites quickly and easily. It was first released in November 2017. Tailwind CSS is a utility-first

CSS framework that is used for rapidly building custom user interfaces. It is a low-level CSS framework that is also highly customizable. It provides the user with all the building blocks they need to create a bespoke design. There are also no existing styles that you need to override in order to personalize and create your website according to your own choices. Tailwind does not impose strict design specifications on the users and hands them free rein so they can create the kind of site they want. For using Tailwind, the user simply needs to bring all these little components together so they can create a site of their liking with a unique interface. Tailwind just takes a raw CSS file and then processes that file over a configuration file and then produces an output.

It is a framework that highly prioritizes utility first with classes like text-focus, flex, pt-4, etc. Using these classes, you can create a website layout straight in your markup. It is increasingly adjustable because it works around utility classes. Working around utility classes also means that we can build custom designs without writing CSS the traditional way. Tailwind also has a faster UI-building process. Using Tailwind ensures that there are minimum lines of code in the CSS file. It also gives us the ability to customize the design and make our own components. It also makes the website responsive and helps us in making the changes in the desired manner. CSS is global in nature, so if you make a single change in a CSS file, it will get implemented in all the places the HTML file is linked with it. However, by using Tailwind CSS you can create local changes by using utility classes.

Features

- Tailwind CSS provides an increased control over styling compared to Bootstrap. As Tailwind does not have a default theme like other CSS frameworks, it becomes easier to style web applications and websites. For example, you can choose to give a different look to each project even if you are using the exact same elements throughout. It is one of the few CSS-based frameworks that are not opinionated about how a user styles their websites and projects.

- When it comes to styling HTML, there is a framework that is faster than Tailwind. You can create amazing looking websites and layouts by styling the elements directly. Tailwind offers thousands of built-in classes which means you don't need to create designs from scratch. You don't need to write any CSS rules by yourself and that is why creating and styling with Tailwind is so fast.

- Tailwind is responsive and also provides additional security. Tailwind is a mobile-friendly CSS framework which allows you to design the layout directly in an HTML file.

- Even though Tailwind CSS is fairly new but it has still proven to be a stable framework since its initial release.

- Tailwind has the ability to create lightweight responsive themes for web applications. It uses PurgeCSS to remove all the unused CSS classes from the final version. This helps in making the final CSS file as small as possible.

JAVASCRIPT

JavaScript is a text-based, interpreted programming or scripting language that allows us to implement complex features on any web page. It is incredibly lightweight and is mostly used for scripting web pages. It is also used to build web applications that interact with the client without reloading the page every time.

The majority of dynamic websites you encounter on the Internet employ at least some JavaScript. JavaScript is used whenever a website displays timely content updates, interactive maps, 2D or 3D graphics, a scrolling movie, or even a simple button that does something when you click on it. The DOM API is used to change the user interface with JavaScript. It accomplishes this by dynamically altering the HTML and CSS.

The acronym DOM stands for Document Object Model. The Document Object Model (DOM) is a cross-platform, language-independent interface that creates a tree structure from HTML text. Each node in the tree represents a document section as an object. A document is represented as a logical tree in the Document Object Model. A node is found at the end of each branch of the tree, and each node contains one item.

The DOM provides programmatic access to a tree, which we can use to alter the tree's structure. Changing the structure of the tree always entails changing the document's inherent behavior. The Document Object Model (DOM) is used to manipulate a page and change its behavior. Not only can the DOM be used to change the document's structure, but it can also be used to change the document's style and content. Attaching event handlers to nodes allows you to control the DOM. An event handler is called whenever an event is triggered.

JavaScript has a massive impact on the Internet.

The impact that JavaScript has on the web is unmatched. It is estimated that more than 97% of the websites available on the Internet use some form of JavaScript on the client-side for displaying any type of web page behavior. In fact, JavaScript is considered one of the essential stepping stones towards learning web development. The prerequisites when it comes to learning JavaScript is a basic understanding of HTML and CSS. One of the things that make JavaScript so popular is the fact that it is versatile and flexible enough to be used in both client-side and server-side.

In real-world applications, DOM produces a document, such as an HTML page, by constructing a tree-like structure within the web browser. Every document's nodes are arranged in a tree structure. A DOM tree is the name for the tree structure. The "document object" is the node at the very top of the tree.

Any browser that renders an HTML page downloads the HTML code into its local memory and then parses it automatically to show the page on the screen. The browser constructs a DOM of the page after it is loaded. The Document Object Model that was constructed would represent the HTML document in an object-oriented manner. It would then serve as a conduit between JavaScript and the document

.A dynamic web page is built in this manner. Any element or its characteristics can be modified, added to, or removed using JavaScript. It can modify any element's CSS style. It can also generate new events while reacting to all existing ones at the same time.

It is common to utilize a DOM tree to show an HTML document, but it is not required. Some browsers do not display documents as trees and instead use internal models. Each browser has its own set of models.

Even though JavaScript is an incredibly versatile language that can be used for almost anything, it is mainly used for creating web-based applications and adding functionality to websites. Other than web apps and web browsers, it is used in servers, software, and even for other hardware controls. JavaScript can be used for things like:

1. **Adding interactive behavior to any web page:** the primary function JavaScript is used for is because it adds interactivity to any web page. It allows the user to interact with the page. There is a lot that you can do with JavaScript that can totally transform a web page. You can add event handlers that get triggered when a certain event occurs. You can choose to show or hide information just on the simple click of a button. It can also change the color of a button when the mouse

hovers over it making it easier for the user to know when they are clicking on a button. This feature can help in many different ways. Like for example if you are making a purchase, you could accidentally click on the buy button which will lead you to buy something that you did not even need in the first place.

2. **Creating web applications:** JavaScript is used for making robust web applications. There are lots of JavaScript frameworks available these days like Angular, React and Vue.js that make it very easy to build complex SPAs. SPA stands for single-page web applications. Developers can easily use these JavaScript frameworks to create mobile apps. A JavaScript framework is simply a collection of a JavaScript code library that would provide the developer with pre-written code. This pre-written available within the framework will help them in creating features and tasks in routine programming. There are lots of popular apps that are made using JavaScript like Netflix, Uber, LinkedIn, etc. There are lots of companies that use Node.js which is a JavaScript based runtime environment. It is built on Google Chrome's JavaScript V8 engine.

3. **Creating mobile apps:** mobile devices are everywhere these days and they are the ones that are used for accessing the Internet by a vast majority of the population. These days most Internet users use their mobile devices to surface the web. JavaScript is so versatile that we can create apps with it that are not even web based in the first place. We can easily build an application for non-web contexts using JavaScript. JavaScript has such varied features that it can be used as a powerful tool for creating web applications. One of the most popular JavaScript-based framework used for creating mobile applications is React Native. React Native allows you to build mobile apps for both Android and iOS that are natively rendered. By using React Native, you can create an application for various platforms by using the same codebase for all of them. We do not need to write different codes for Android and iOS. React Native follows "WORA" which stands for Write Once, Run Anywhere. WORA is used to describe the ability of a program to be just written once and then run on any platform. This term was first coined by Sun Microsystems in reference to Java.

4. **Building web servers:** a web server can easily be created using Node.j s. Node.js is an open source, cross-platform, backend-based runtime

environment in JavaScript. It runs on Google Chrome's JavaScript V8 engine and helps us in executing JavaScript code outside of a web browser. With node.js you can write command line tools. And when you are doing server-side scripting, you can run your script on the server-side and produce dynamic web page content. You can do all of this without even sending the page to the web browser of the user. Using node.js also helps in maintaining the "JavaScript everywhere" paradigm for developers. This paradigm is based on the fact that all the core components of the web application are unified and created in one single language rather than multiple different languages, for server-side and client-side scripts separately.

5. **Developing server applications:** most of the web applications that we use these days have a server-side to them. A server is useful when it comes to dynamically display data as required. For example, let us say there is an online shopping website, now imagine how many products would be available on any given shopping website. If we start displaying all the data for each product using static pages, not just would it be incredibly inefficient but also incredibly time consuming. So instead, what most of the sites do is they display static templates that are built using HTML, CSS, and JavaScript and then they dynamically update the data inside those templates as per their requirement. When you want to view a different product than what you were originally viewing, the data inside the template will change as it would pull data from the server to display data of the product that you want to see. JavaScript helps in generating content and handling HTTP requests. JavaScript can run on servers as well by using Node.js. Node.js provides an environment that contains all the necessary tools that are required to run JavaScript on a web server.

6. **Developing games:** JavaScript can also be used for creating games. You can easily create a browser game using JavaScript. In fact, creating a game using JavaScript is a great way for beginners to test their skills. JavaScript has lots of libraries and frameworks that can be used for creating a game. You can easily create a 2D or a 3D game using JavaScript. You can also create a top-quality game with JavaScript. It is the kind of language that has so many libraries and frameworks, so it is rather expected that it would have tons of game engine options as well. You can choose from all these different game

engine options that would fit your programming skills and needs. These game engines are not just free and open source but many of them even work well within a web editor and provide incredibly fast rendering for 2D and 3D elements. Fast rendering of the graphics is a very important aspect of any type of game. Some of the popular JavaScript game engines are Phaser, Babylon.js, Cocos2D, PlayCanvas, Kiwi.js, Panda Engine, Pixi.js, etc.

7. **Web development:** JavaScript is one of the most important step for anyone that wants to become a web developer. JavaScript is most popularly used for making interactive web pages. It helps us in adding dynamic behavior to a web page. It also helps us in adding any kind of special effects to any type of web page. On most websites, JavaScript helps with the validation purposes. JavaScript helps us in executing some complex actions that makes the clients easily interact with the websites. By using JavaScript, a website can possibly load content into a document without even loading the web page.

8. **Presentations:** JavaScript is also capable of creating presentations as a website. There are various such libraries available that can help us create a web-based slide deck like RevealJS, BespokeJS, etc. They are relatively easy to use, so you can easily create something incredible in a very short span of time. Reveal.js is mostly used to create interactive and beautiful slide decks. It works with some help from HTML. These presentations work not only well on desktop but also on mobile devices and tablets as well. It also supports all kinds of CSS color formats. On the other hand, BespokeJS includes a wide variety of features like bullet lists, responsive scaling, etc.

Pros

- JavaScript always gets executed on the client-side regardless of where you host it. It saves lots of bandwidth and makes the execution process faster.

- XMLHttpRequest is an important object in JavaScript that was designed by Microsoft. The object call that is made by XMLHttpRequest is an asynchronous HTTP request made to the server. It helps in transferring data to both sides without reloading a page.

- One of the biggest advantages of JavaScript is that it has the ability to support all modern browsers. It also produces an equivalent result in every browser.

- JavaScript also receives support from the biggest companies in the world by creating projects. Like Google created Angular framework, in the same way, Facebook (now Meta) created the React.js framework.

- It is ubiquitous as it is used everywhere on the web.

- It works great with other languages as well thus, it can be utilized in various types of applications.

- There are lots of open-source projects available that help the developer.

- Lots of community support and courses available online to learn JavaScript easily and quickly.

- It allows creation of rich interfaces.

- It is versatile, so you can create a whole JavaScript app from front end to back end using just JavaScript.

Cons

- It may be difficult to develop large applications solely on the basis of JavaScript. You might have to use the TypeScript overlay.

- It is applied to mostly large frontend projects. The configuration is tedious as the number of tools that are required to create an environment for such a project is a lot. That is why it is sometimes directly associated with the library's operation.

- The main disadvantage of JavaScript is that the code can be viewed by anyone.

- No matter how fast JavaScript interprets, the DOM (Document Object Model) is comparatively slow and can never render fast enough with HTML.

- If some error occurs in the JavaScript, then it can even stop the whole website. And this happens even though the browsers are extremely tolerant of errors in JavaScript.

- It is usually interpreted differently by different browsers. This makes it somewhat complex to read and write the browser code.

- Even though some HTML editors do provide the debugging feature, it is still not as efficient as other editors for languages like C and C++. This makes detecting the problem harder for the developer.

- The conversions take a longer time when converting a number to an integer. This not just increases the time needed to run the script but also reduces the overall speed.

Let's talk about JS frameworks now. A framework is a tool that provides ready-made components that can be customized by the user. They are generally used to speed up the development process while providing standard and low-level functionality. Using a framework increases the software reliability while also simplifying testing and reducing the overall programming time. It can have support programs, compilers, toolsets, APIs, and libraries in order to create systems and develop software. A JavaScript framework is written in JavaScript and can be used by the developers to manipulate the functions and customize it according to their needs. Frameworks are increasingly adaptable when it comes to designing websites so most frontend developers prefer using it. Using a framework makes working with JS much easier and smoother. It also helps the developer code the application in such a way that it is responsive irrespective of the device. Now let's take a look at some of the most popular JS frameworks used for frontend development.

REACTJS

ReactJS or simply React is the most used frontend-based JS framework. It is also free and open source and is used for building dynamic user interfaces based on UI components. It was developed and currently maintained by Meta, formerly known as Facebook. It is capable of creating and handling web pages with high incoming traffic. React is mostly used for state management and rendering that state to DOM. It uses virtual DOM and integrates the same with any other application. React does the manipulation with the virtual DOM in the memory before it makes any final changes within the DOM of the browser. It is done so that it only changes what needs to be changed. React was first released for public use in July 2013 and was created by Jordan Walke.

Characteristics

- React is used to create dynamic and interactive UI for mobile and web applications. It is also capable of rendering the right components efficiently in case there is a change in network speed.

- It has declarative views that make the code readable and incredibly easy to debug.

- For every DOM object, React creates a virtual DOM object. A virtual DOM object is created by making a virtual copy of the original DOM and is used as a representation of the primary DOM.

- React has a W3C object model event system that is also fully compatible.

- React also provides cross-browser interface to any native event. It means you don't need to worry about incompatible event names and fields.

- JSX is a markup syntax that makes writing React components easier. It makes the syntax almost identical to the HTML injected into the web page.

- React uses an application architecture called flux controls. React updates the view for the user and Flux controls the application workflow. Virtual DOM will compare the new data with the original data and update the view automatically.

- React Native is used as a custom renderer for React and it makes use of the native components instead of the web components.

- Everything is seen as a component of the web page in React. A view or the UI is created by combining all the components together. A component is used to define the visuals in ReactJS.

Angular

Angular is a frontend-based web application framework written in TypeScript. It is free, open-source and it is operated by Google. Angular is also part of the MEAN stack. Apart from Angular, MEAN stack uses MongoDB database, Express.js as a web application server framework and Node.js as a server runtime environment. Angular is mostly used for developing a single-page application also called an SPA. Angular extends the HTML into the application and interprets the attributes in such a way as to perform data binding.

Features

- Capable of delivering app-like experience through a web platform while also maintaining a high standard of performance.

- No installation is required for such web apps and can also provide the functionality to work offline.

- Usage of strategies from Cordova, Ionic, or NativeScript to build a native app.

- Using the same methods to create a web app, desktop-installed apps can also be created for Mac, Windows, and Linux.

- Angular can turn templates into code that is highly optimized and gives the benefits of handwritten code.

- Capable of serving the first view of .NET, PHP, Node.js, and other similar servers for almost instant rendering in HTML and CSS.

- Angular apps load quickly and deliver automatic code-splitting so users can load the code they require to render the view they request.

- Angular can easily create UI views with a simple yet powerful template syntax.

- Angular command-line tools help in building apps quickly, adding required components fast, and instantly deploy them.

- Angular is popular enough, so most IDEs and editors provide intelligent code completion, and instant error feedback.

- Protractor helps in making scenario tests run faster and in a stable manner.

- Angular's intuitive API helps in creating high-performance animation timelines with very little code.

- Angular helps in creating accessible applications that have ARIA-enabled components and developer guides for the same.

Advantages of Frontend Development

- It provides quick development because of all the available modern frameworks and innovations. As the front end is built quickly, the journey towards the final product also becomes shorter.

- It provides a secure coding environment. Entire set of code and the whole website is secure on any browser.

- Frameworks allow developers to create quick responding features that make the application work smooth and fast and respond well.

- The tools and techniques are easy to learn. Most of the frontend development is limited to the three core technologies that are HTML, CSS, and JavaScript.

- It provides robust features and a scalable environment.

Disadvantages of Frontend Development

- One of the biggest issues is code inflation. No matter how big or small a website is, customization is an essential part. In order to do that, the frameworks that are used for building the website indirectly led to a bigger codebase.

- Compared to the languages used at the backend like PHP and Java which have been around for quite some time now, JavaScript is fairly new. Even though it is an essential component of front end, the relatable and long-term knowledge is very limited.

- Newer version of frontend frameworks and libraries keep on releasing in quick succession. The continued fresh and major updates are more of a hassle as with the new versions there is a bigger chance of messing up.

CHAPTER SUMMARY

In this chapter, we took a brief overview of all the things that we have learned in the past. It provides a bird's eye view of all the major topics and technologies used for frontend development. This chapter was just a way to go through the key points of frontend development and see for ourselves why it is beneficial to us.

Bibliography

Awati, R. (2022, January 1). *What is Asynchronous JavaScript and XML (AJAX)?* https://www.theserverside.com/definition/Ajax-Asynchronous-JavaScript-and-XML

Bootstrap (Front-End Framework) - Wikipedia. (2017, February 1). https://en.wikipedia.org/wiki/Bootstrap_(front-end_framework). Last edited on September 27, 2022.

Client-Server Model – GeeksforGeeks. (2019, October 23). https://www.geeksforgeeks.org/client-server-model/#:~:text=Advantages%20of%20Client-Server%20model%3A%20Centralized%20system%20with%20all,less%20maintenance%20cost%20and%20Data%20recovery%20is%20possible

The Client/Server Model. (2021, March 22). https://www.ibm.com/docs/en/zos/2.2.0?topic=applications-clientserver-model

Code Optimization | Code Optimization Techniques | Gate Vidyalay. (2018, March 14). https://www.gatevidyalay.com/code-optimization-techniques/#:~:text=In%20Compiler%20design%2C%20Code%20Optimization%20is%20an%20approach,Code%20movement%2C%20Dead%20code%20elimination%2C%20Strength%20reduction.%20Author

Code Optimization in Compiler Design. (2017, September 26). GeeksforGeeks. https://www.geeksforgeeks.org/code-optimization-in-compiler-design/

Code Optimization Study Notes: Know the types, different ways to Code Optimization. (n.d.). Retrieved July 10, 2022, from https://byjusexamprep.com/code-optimization-study-notes-i

CodeHawke | CSS & SASS. (n.d.). Retrieved July 10, 2022, from https://www.codehawke.com/css_and_sass.html#:~:text=Sass%20is%20short%20for%20Syntactically%20Awesome%20Style%20Sheets,indented%20syntax%2C%22%20uses%20a%20syntax%20similar%20to%20Haml

CSS. (1996, December 17). Wikipedia. https://en.wikipedia.org/wiki/CSS#:~:text=Cascading%20Style%20Sheets%20%28CSS%29%20is%20a%20style%20sheet,World%20Wide%20Web%2C%20alongside%20HTML%20and%20JavaScript.%20. Last edited on September 23, 2022.

CSS RGB and RGBA Colors. (n.d.). Retrieved July 10, 2022, from https://www.w3schools.com/Css/css_colors_rgb.asp

CSS: Cascading Style Sheets. (2022, May 2). MDN. https://developer.mozilla.org/en-US/docs/Web/CSS

Dhawan, S. (2018, May 13). *What's New in CSS 3. WHAT IS CSS? | by Sahil Dhawan | Beginner's Guide to Mobile Web Development.* Medium. https://medium.com/beginners-guide-to-mobile-web-development/whats-new-in-css-3-dcd7fa6122e1

The Document Metadata (Header) Element - HTML: HyperText Markup Language. (2022, February 18). MDN. https://developer.mozilla.org/en-US/docs/Web/HTML/Element/head

DOM (Document Object Model). (2018, June 6). GeeksforGeeks. https://www.geeksforgeeks.org/dom-document-object-model/

EDUCBA. (n.d.). What is Packet Switching? Retrieved July 10, 2022, from https://www.educba.com/what-is-packet-switching/#:~:text=The%20email%20is%20sent%20through%20the%20network%20as,the%20packets%20are%20assembled%20to%20the%20original%20format

Frontend Development vs Backend Development. (2022, January 5). Blogs | Engineer Master Solutions LLC - You Think, We Deliver. https://blog.engineermaster.co/frontend-development-vs-backend-development/#:~:text=Web%20development%20also%20has%20two%20parts%20front%20end,the%20content%20of%20any%20website%20to%20the%20end-users

How does JavaScript Work. (n.d.). javatpoint. Retrieved July 10, 2022, from https://www.javatpoint.com/how-does-javascript-work

Html - HTML - W3cubDocs. (n.d.). Retrieved July 10, 2022, from https://docs.w3cub.com/html/element/html.html

HTTP - HyperText Transfer Protocol. (n.d.). javatpoint. Retrieved July 10, 2022, from https://www.javatpoint.com/computer-network-http

Indeed Editorial Team. (2021, July 22). *Indeed.* What is the Client-Server Model? (Plus Definition and Functions). The Client/Server Model. (2021, March 22). The Client/Server Model. https://www.ibm.com/docs/en/zos/2.2.0?topic=applications-clientserver-model

Internet. (2021, January 1). Wikipedia. https://en.wikipedia.org/wiki/Internet. Last edited on September 28, 2022.

Introduction to Tailwind CSS. (2020, June 24). GeeksforGeeks. https://www.geeksforgeeks.org/introduction-to-tailwind-css/

JavaScript. (n.d.). GeeksforGeeks. Retrieved July 10, 2022, from https://www.geeksforgeeks.org/javascript/

JavaScript Library. (2018, January 15). Wikipedia. https://en.wikipedia.org/wiki/JavaScript_library. Last edited on August 7, 2022.

Javascript Tutorial. (n.d.). Retrieved July 10, 2022, from https://www.tutorialspoint.com/javascript/

Javascript Tutorial. (n.d.). Retrieved July 10, 2022, from https://www.tutorialspoint.com/javascript/

Learn Stylus in Y Minutes. (n.d.). Retrieved July 10, 2022, from https://learnxinyminutes.com/docs/stylus/#:~:text=Stylus%20is%20a%20dynamic%20stylesheet%20preprocessor%20language%20that,this%20using%20%20variables%2C%20nesting%2C%20mixins%2C%20functions%20and%20%20more

Ledbetter, L. (1997, January 10). *What is Metadata?* Webopedia. https://www
.webopedia.com/definitions/metadata/#:~:text=Metadata%20is%20data
%20that%20provides%20information%20about%20other,management
%2C%20or%20other%20context%20of%20the%20data%20content

Less (Stylesheet Language). (2009, January 1). Wikipedia. https://en.wikipedia
.org/wiki/Less_(stylesheet_language)#:~:text=Less%20%28Leaner%20
Style%20Sheets%3B%20sometimes%20stylized%20as%20LESS%29,on%20
the%20client%20side%20or%20server%20side.%20. Last edited on July 19,
2022.

MDN Web Docs. (n.d.). Retrieved July 10, 2022, from https://developer.mozilla
.org/en-US/

The Most Advanced Responsive Front-End Framework in the World. (n.d.).
Foundation. Retrieved July 10, 2022, from https://get.foundation/

Pseudo-classes - The Basics - SitePoint. (n.d.). Retrieved July 10, 2022, from https://
www.sitepoint.com/pseudo-classes-the-basics/

Sarosa, A. (2018, November 15). *What is HTML? Hypertext Markup Language
Basics for Beginners.* Hostinger Tutorials. https://www.hostinger.com/tuto-
rials/what-is-html

Siddhapura, Y. (2022, March 1). *What are the CSS Preprocessors? | Preprocessors
in Action | SASS | Less.* Bigscal - Outsource Software Development Services.
https://www.bigscal.com/blogs/frontend-technology/what-are-css-pre-
processors/#:~:text=CSS%20preprocessors%20are%20added%20their
%20functionality%20those%20not,mixin%2C%20nesting%20selector%2C
%20inheritance%20selector%2C%20and%20so%20on

TCP/IP in Computer Networking. (2020, May 31). GeeksforGeeks. https://www
.geeksforgeeks.org/tcp-ip-in-computer-networking/#:~:text=TCP%2FIP
%20employs%20the%20client-server%20demonstration%20of%20com-
munication%20in,by%20another%20computer%20%28a%20server%29
%20within%20the%20network

TCP/IP: What is TCP/IP and How Does it Work? (2021, July 1). SearchNetworking.
https://www.techtarget.com/searchnetworking/definition/TCP-IP

W3Schools. (n.d.). HTML <link> Tag. Retrieved July 10, 2022, from https://www
.w3schools.com/Tags/tag_link.asp#:~:text=Definition%20and%20Usage
%20The%20%3Clink%3E%20tag%20defines%20the,or%20to%20add%20a
%20favicon%20to%20your%20website

W3Schools Free Online Web Tutorials. (n.d.). W3Schools Online Web Tutorials.
Retrieved July 10, 2022, from https://www.w3schools.com/

What are the Four Layers in the TCP/IP Reference Model? (2020, September 2).
https://itexamanswers.net/question/what-are-the-four-layers-in-the-tcp
-ip-reference-model#:~:text=Explanation%3A%20The%20TCP%2FIP
%20model%20has%20four%20layers.%20Each,bottom%20are%20appli-
cation%2C%20transport%2C%20internet%2C%20and%20network
%20access

What are the Pros and Cons of Frontend Web Development. (2019, June 20).
Nextscrum. https://www.nextscrum.com/what-are-the-pros-and-cons-of
-frontend-web-development/

What is a CSS Framework? (2022, March 8). Elementor. https://elementor.com/resources/glossary/what-is-a-css-framework/

What is an Intranet? Definition, Benefits and Features. (2021, September 1). https://www.techtarget.com/whatis/definition/intranet

What is an IP Address & What does it mean? (2022, April 18). https://www.kaspersky.com/resource-center/definitions/what-is-an-ip-address

What is Code Optimization and its Types? (2018, March 26). Apachebooster Blog: Showcasing the Tech Blogs Written by Our Writers. https://apache-booster.com/blog/what-is-code-optimization-and-its-types/#:~:text=Code%20optimization%2C%20as%20the%20name%20indicates%20can%20be,execute%20more%20rapidly%2C%20or%20performs%20fewer%20opera-tions%20%28input%2Foutput%29

What is Hypertext Transfer Protocol Secure (HTTPS)? (2022, March 1). https://www.techtarget.com/searchsoftwarequality/definition/HTTPS

What is JavaScript? - Learn Web Development. (2022, March 23). MDN. https://developer.mozilla.org/en-US/docs/Learn/JavaScript/First_steps/What_is_JavaScript

What is the Difference between Webpage, Website, Web Server, and Search Engine? - Learn Web Development. (2022, April 27). MDN. https://developer.mozilla.org/en-US/docs/Learn/Common_questions/Pages_sites_servers_and_search_engines?retiredLocale=id

Index

Printed in the United States
by Baker & Taylor Publisher Services